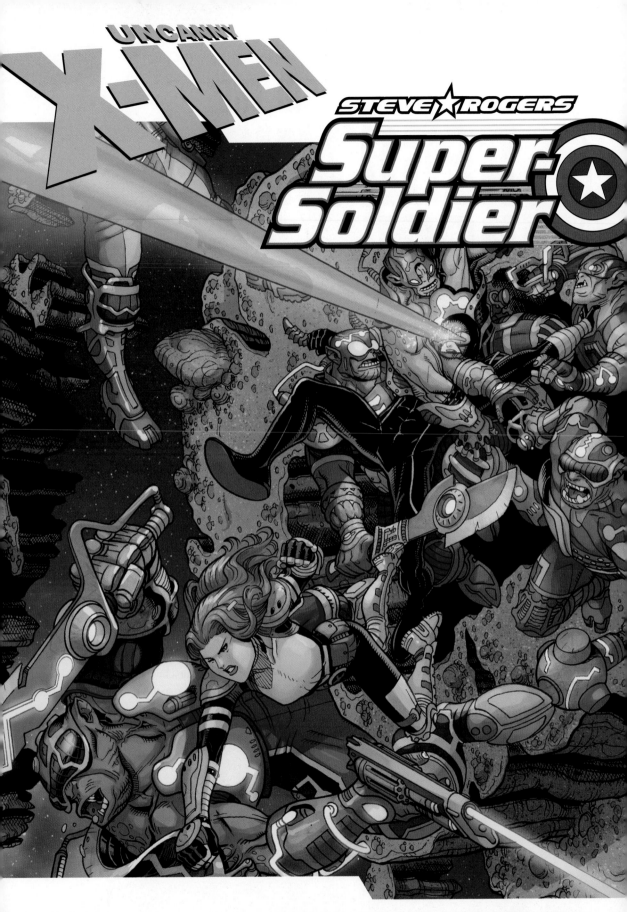

X-MEN/STEVE ROGERS: ESCAPE FROM THE NEGATIVE ZONE. Contains material originally published in magazine form as UNCANNY X-MEN ANNUAL #3, STEVE ROGERS: SUPER-SOLDIER ANNUAL #1 and AMOR: THE FIRST MUTANT ANNUAL #1. First printing 2011. ISBN# 978-0-7851-5560-7. Published by MARVEL WORLDWIDE, INC., a subsidiary of MARVEL ENTERTAINMENT, LLC. OFFICE OF PUBLICATION: 135 West 50th Street, New York, NY 10020. Copyright © 2011 Marvel Characters, Inc. All rights reserved. $19.99 per copy in the U.S. and $21.99 in Canada (GST #R127032852); Canadian Agreement #40668537. All characters featured in this issue and the distinctive names and likenesses thereof, and all related indicia are trademarks of Marvel Characters, Inc. No similarity between any of the names, characters, persons, and/or institutions in this magazine with those of any living or dead person or institution is intended, and any such similarity which may exist is purely coincidental. **Printed in the U.S.A.** ALAN FINE, EVP - Office of the President, Marvel Worldwide, Inc. and EVP & CMO Marvel Characters B.V.; DAN BUCKLEY, Publisher & President - Print, Animation & Digital Divisions; JOE QUESADA, Chief Creative Officer; JIM SOKOLOWSKI, Chief Operating Officer; DAVID BOGART, SVP of Business Affairs & Talent Management; TOM BREVOORT, SVP of Publishing; C.B. CEBULSKI, SVP of Creator & Content Development; DAVID GABRIEL, SVP of Publishing Sales & Circulation; MICHAEL PASCIULLO, SVP of Brand Planning & Communications; JIM O'KEEFE, VP of Operations & Logistics; DAN CARR, Executive Director of Publishing Technology; JUSTIN F. GABRIE, Director of Publishing & Editorial Operations; SUSAN CRESPI, Editorial Operations Manager; ALEX MORALES, Publishing Operations Manager; STAN LEE, Chairman Emeritus. For information regarding advertising in Marvel Comics or on Marvel.com, please contact John Dokes, SVP Integrated Sales and Marketing, at jdokes@marvel.com. For Marvel subscription inquiries, please call 800-217-9158. Manufactured between 6/6/11 and 7/4/11 by R.R. DONNELLEY, INC., SALEM, VA, USA.

10987654321

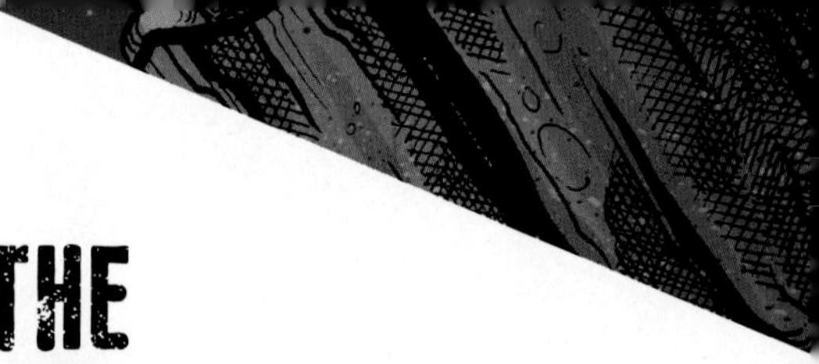

ESCAPE FROM THE NEGATIVE ZONE

Writer: **James Asmus**

Artist, *Uncanny X-Men Annual #3*: **Nick Bradshaw**

Artist, *Steve Rogers: Super-Soldier Annual #1*: **Ibraim Roberson**

Artist, *Namor: The First Mutant Annual #1*: **Max Fiumara**

with ink assist from **Norman Lee**

Colorist: **Jim Charalampidis**

Letterer: **Jared K. Fletcher**

Cover Artist: **Black Frog**

Assistant Editors: **Jake Thomas** & **Jordan D. White**

Associate Editor: **Daniel Ketchum**

Editor: **Nick Lowe**

Collection Editor & Design: **Cory Levine**

Editorial Assistants: **James Emmett** & **Joe Hochstein**

Assistant Editors: **Matt Masdeu**, **Alex Starbuck** & **Nelson Ribeiro**

Editors, Special Projects: **Jennifer Grünwald** & **Mark D. Beazley**

Senior Editor, Special Projects: **Jeff Youngquist**

Senior Vice President of Sales: **David Gabriel**

SVP of Brand Planning & Communications: **Michael Pasciullo**

Collection Cover Artists: **Nick Bradshaw** & **Jim Charalampidis**

Editor In Chief: **Axel Alonso**

Chief Creative Officer: **Joe Quesada**

Publisher: **Dan Buckley**

Executive Producer: **Alan Fine**

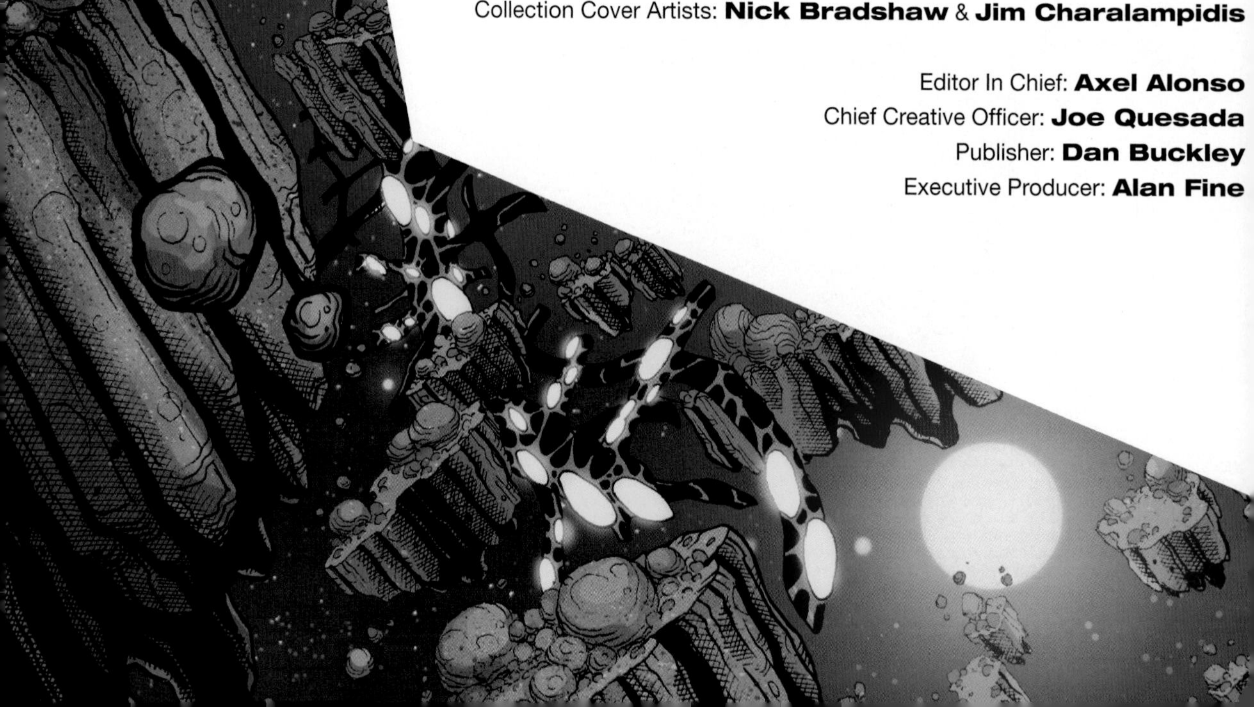

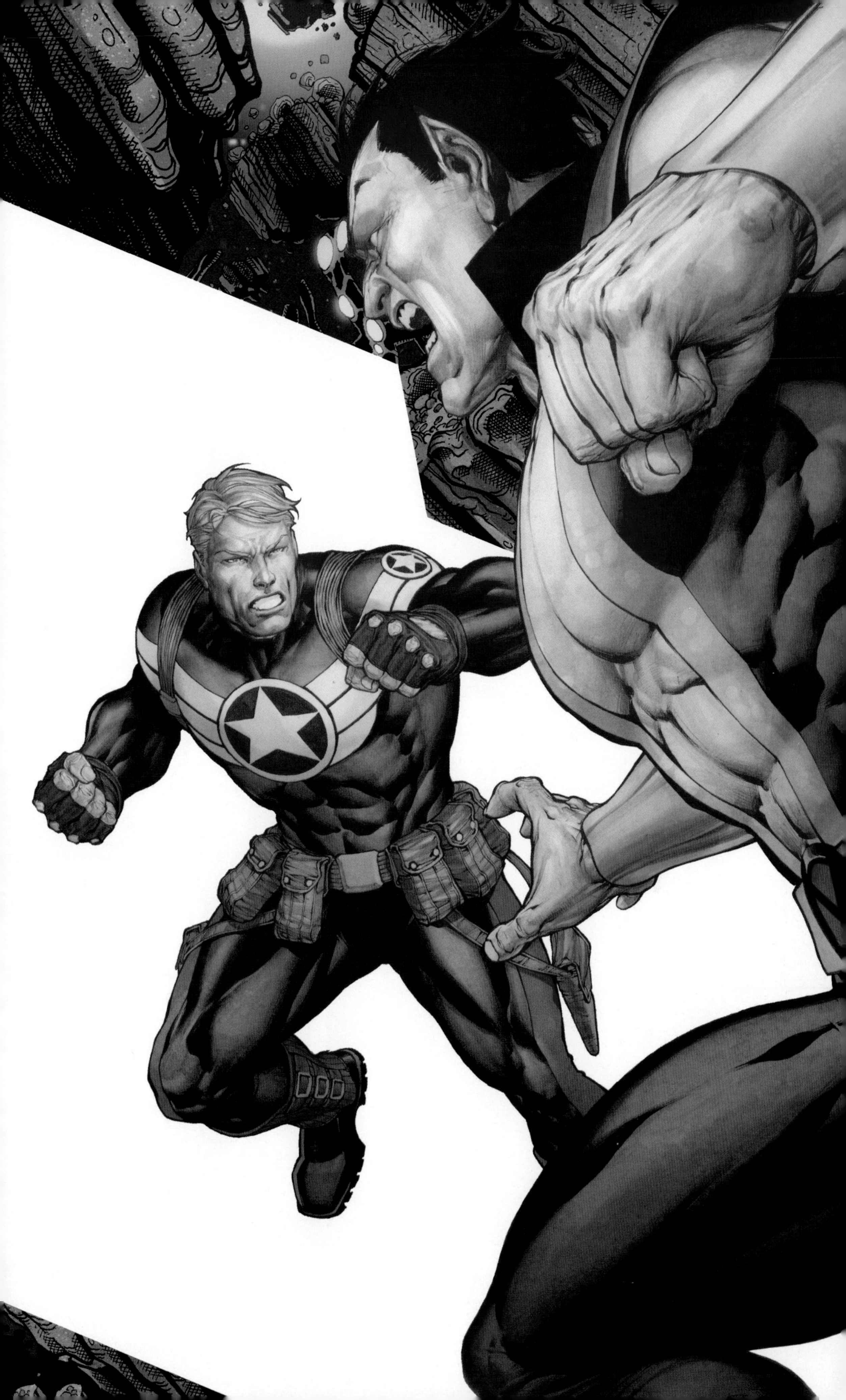

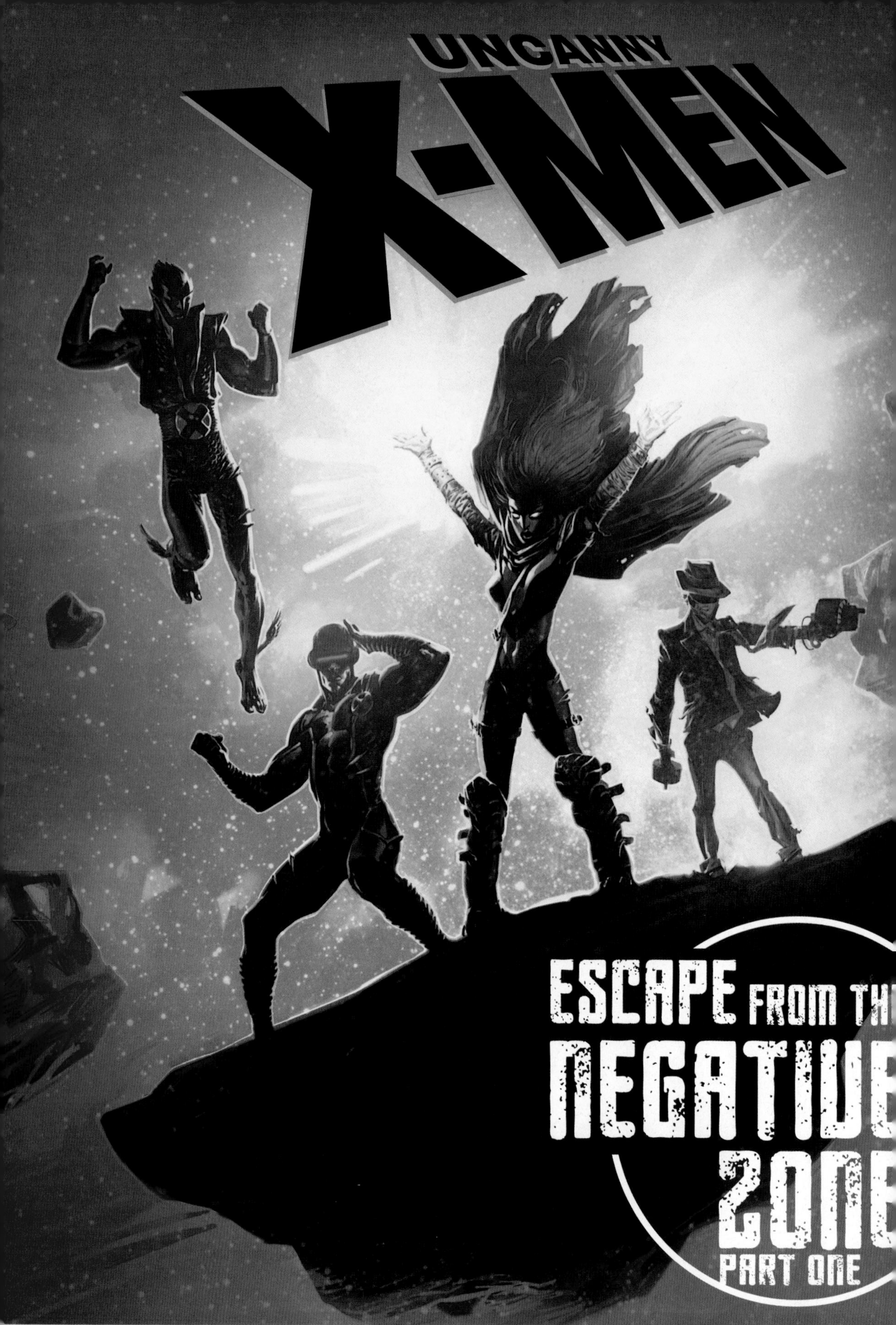

ANNUAL #03 2011

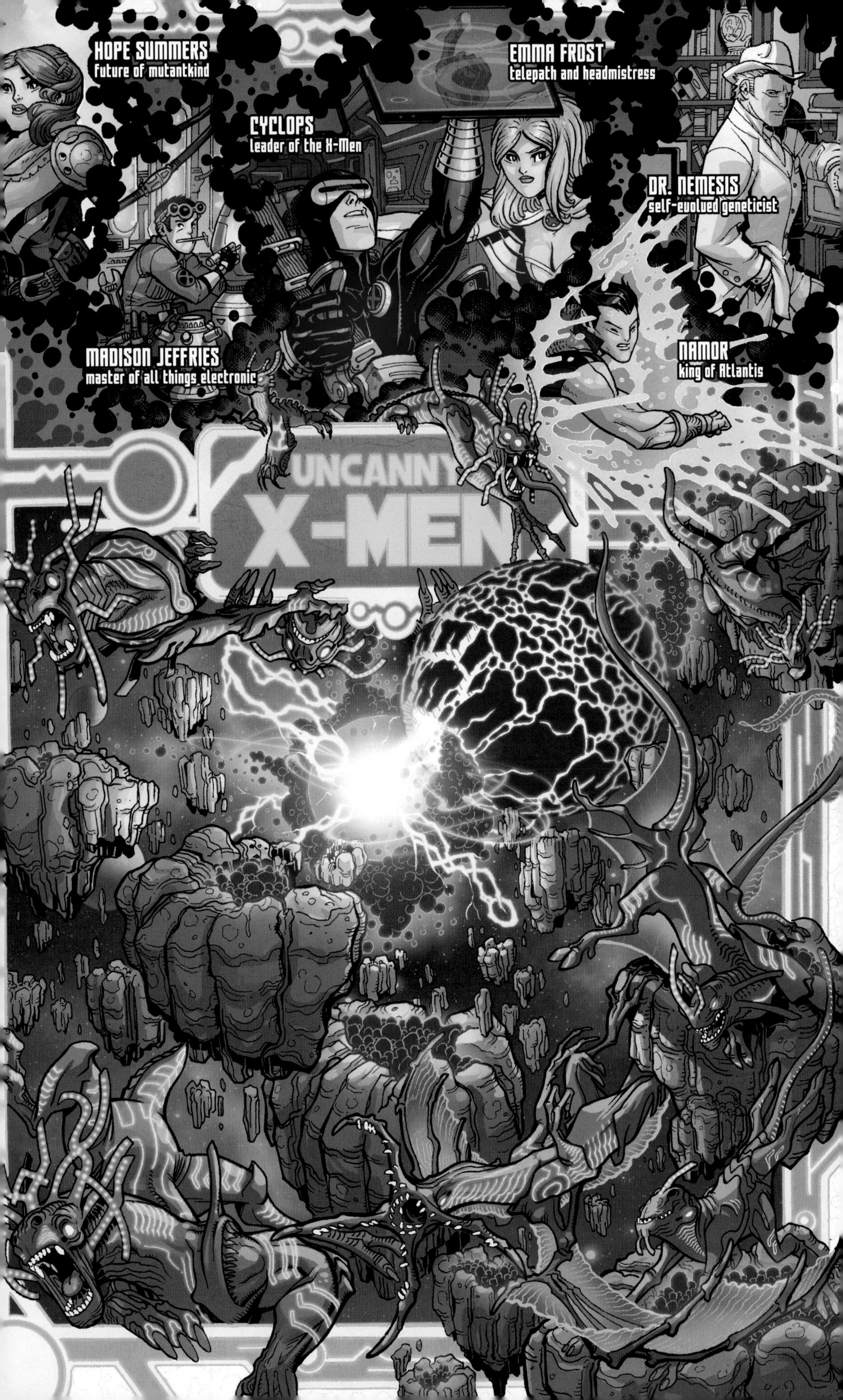
HOPE SUMMERS
future of mutantkind
EMMA FROST
telepath and headmistress
CYCLOPS
leader of the X-Men
DR. NEMESIS
self-evolved geneticist
MADISON JEFFRIES
master of all things electronic
NAMOR
king of Atlantis
UNCANNY
X-MEN

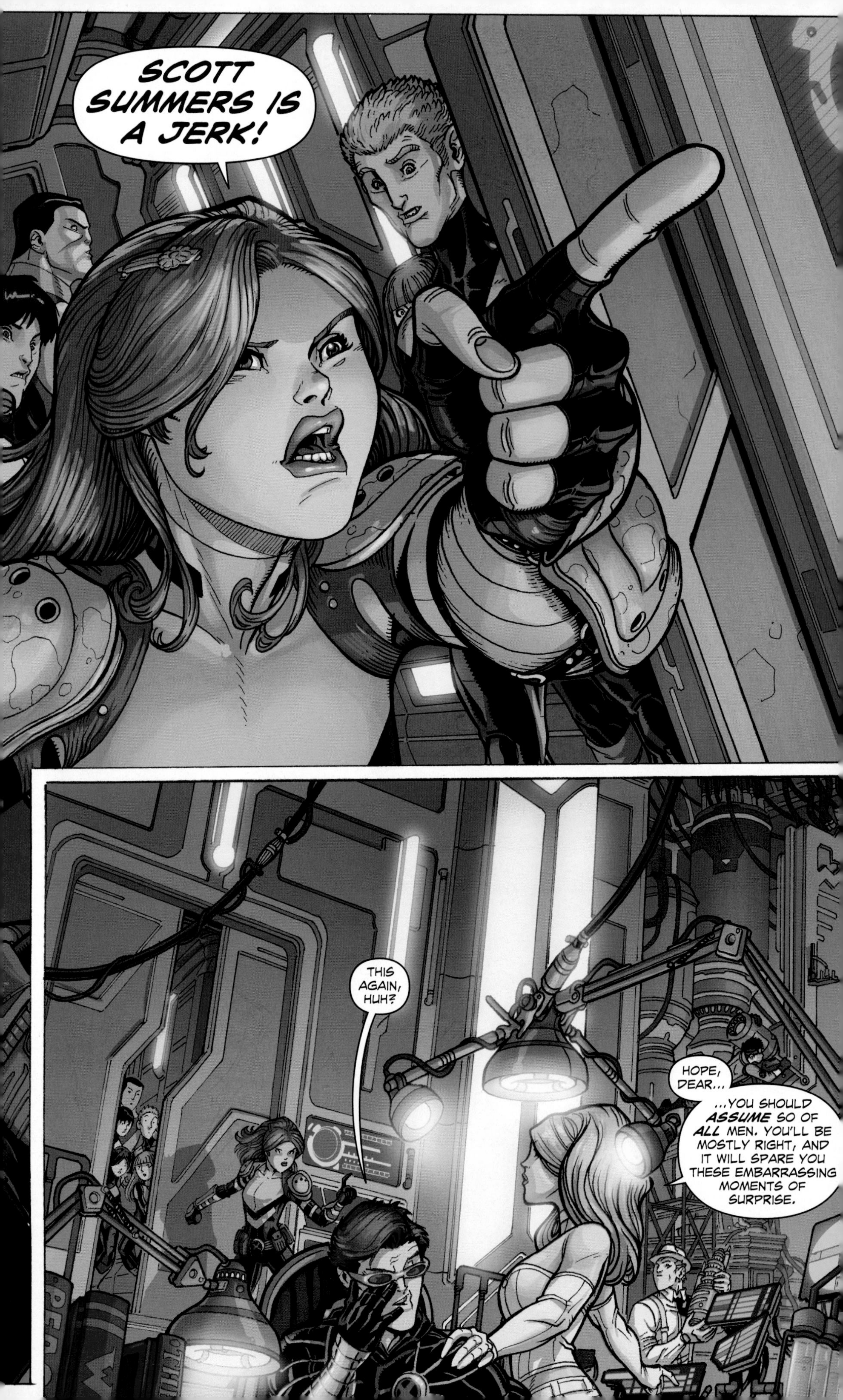
SCOTT SUMMERS IS A JERK!
THIS AGAIN, HUH?
HOPE, DEAR...
...YOU SHOULD ASSUME SO OF ALL MEN. YOU'LL BE MOSTLY RIGHT, AND IT WILL SPARE YOU THESE EMBARRASSING MOMENTS OF SURPRISE.

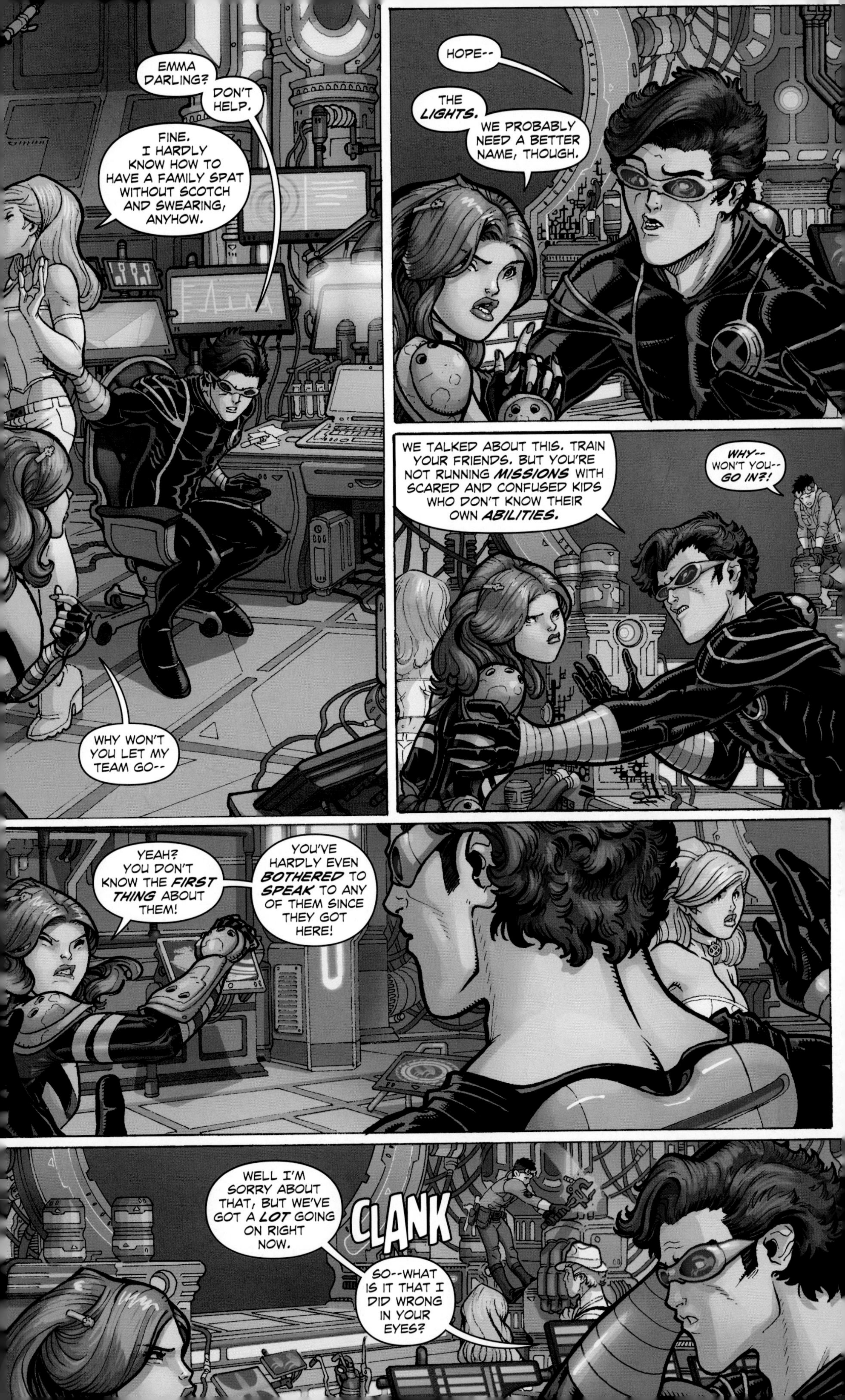
EMMA DARLING?
DON'T HELP.
FINE. I HARDLY KNOW HOW TO HAVE A FAMILY SPAT WITHOUT SCOTCH AND SWEARING, ANYHOW.
WHY WON'T YOU LET MY TEAM GO--
HOPE--
THE LIGHTS.
WE PROBABLY NEED A BETTER NAME, THOUGH.
WE TALKED ABOUT THIS. TRAIN YOUR FRIENDS. BUT YOU'RE NOT RUNNING MISSIONS WITH SCARED AND CONFUSED KIDS WHO DON'T KNOW THEIR OWN ABILITIES.
WHY-- WON'T YOU-- GO IN?!
YEAH? YOU DON'T KNOW THE FIRST THING ABOUT THEM!
YOU'VE HARDLY EVEN BOTHERED TO SPEAK TO ANY OF THEM SINCE THEY GOT HERE!
WELL I'M SORRY ABOUT THAT, BUT WE'VE GOT A LOT GOING ON RIGHT NOW.
CLANK
SO--WHAT IS IT THAT I DID WRONG IN YOUR EYES?

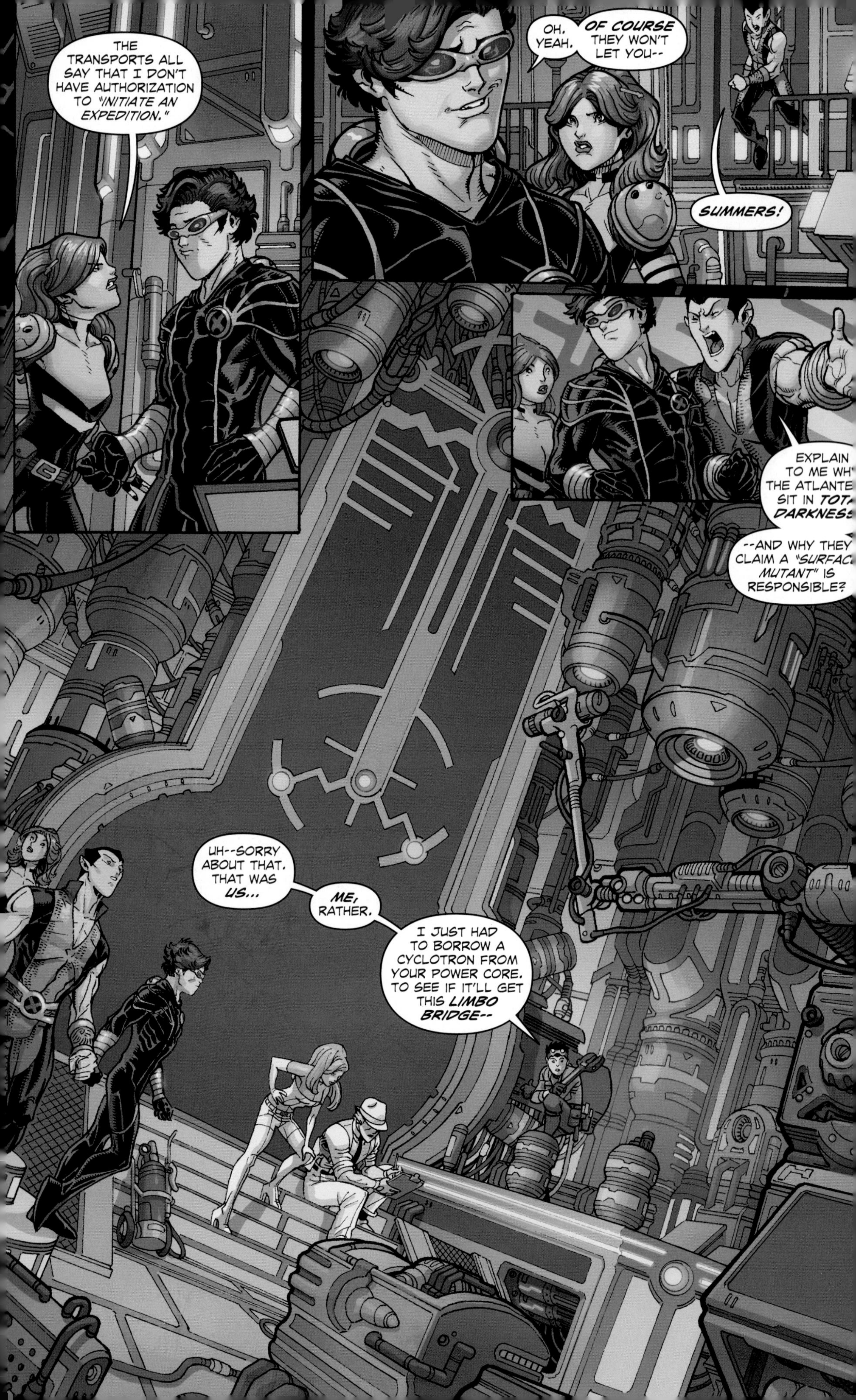
THE TRANSPORTS ALL SAY THAT I DON'T HAVE AUTHORIZATION TO "INITIATE AN EXPEDITION."
OH. YEAH.
OF COURSE THEY WON'T LET YOU--
SUMMERS!
EXPLAIN TO ME WHY THE ATLANTE SIT IN TOTA DARKNESS
--AND WHY THEY CLAIM A "SURFAC MUTANT" IS RESPONSIBLE?
UH--SORRY ABOUT THAT. THAT WAS US...
ME, RATHER.
I JUST HAD TO BORROW A CYCLOTRON FROM YOUR POWER CORE. TO SEE IF IT'LL GET THIS LIMBO BRIDGE--

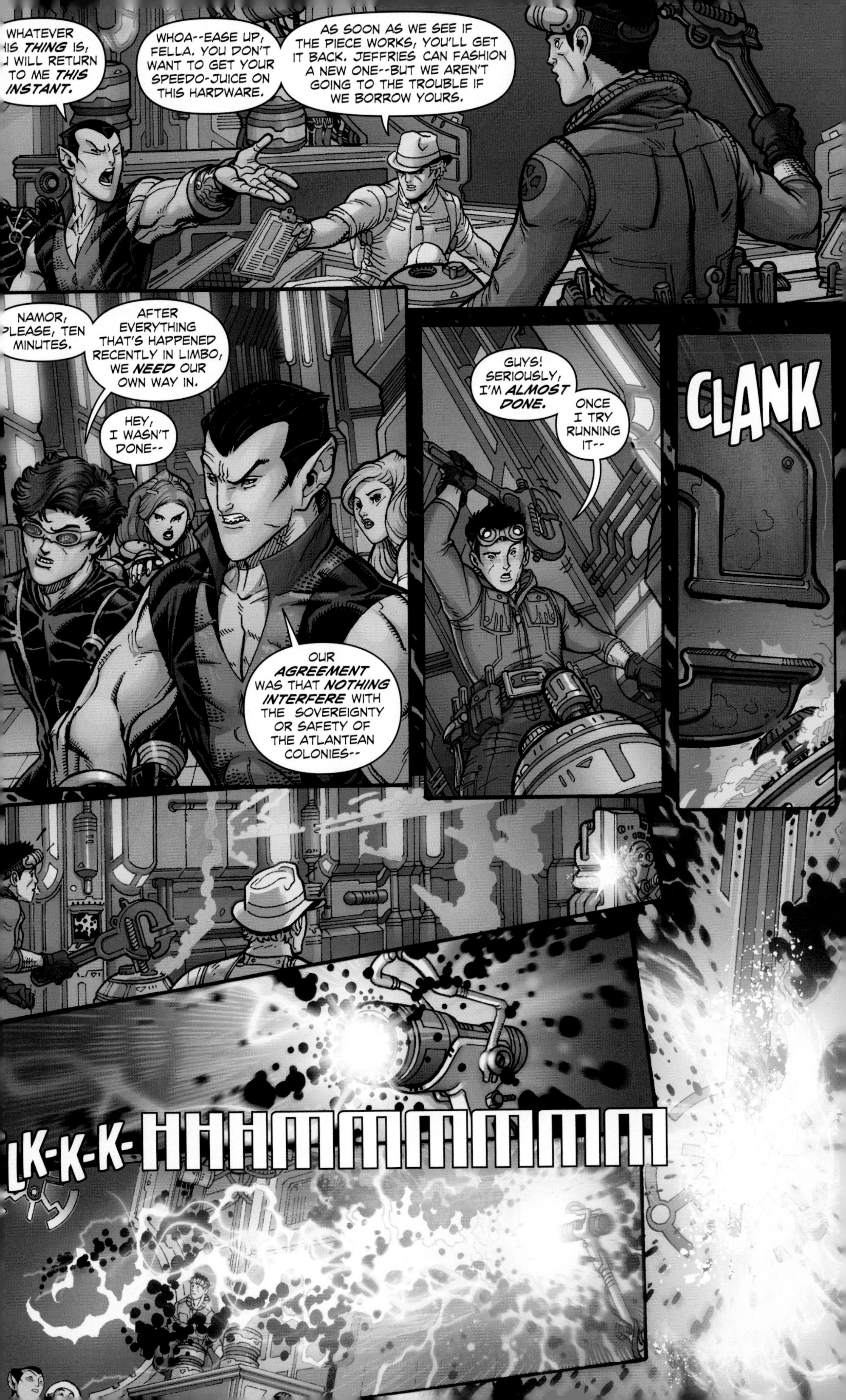
WHATEVER THIS THING IS, I WILL RETURN TO ME THIS INSTANT.
WHOA--EASE UP, FELLA. YOU DON'T WANT TO GET YOUR SPEEDO-JUICE ON THIS HARDWARE.
AS SOON AS WE SEE IF THE PIECE WORKS, YOU'LL GET IT BACK. JEFFRIES CAN FASHION A NEW ONE--BUT WE AREN'T GOING TO THE TROUBLE IF WE BORROW YOURS.
NAMOR, PLEASE, TEN MINUTES.
AFTER EVERYTHING THAT'S HAPPENED RECENTLY IN LIMBO, WE NEED OUR OWN WAY IN.
HEY, I WASN'T DONE--
OUR AGREEMENT WAS THAT NOTHING INTERFERE WITH THE SOVEREIGNTY OR SAFETY OF THE ATLANTEAN COLONIES--
GUYS! SERIOUSLY, I'M ALMOST DONE.
ONCE I TRY RUNNING IT--
CLANK
LK-K-K-HHHMMMMMMMM

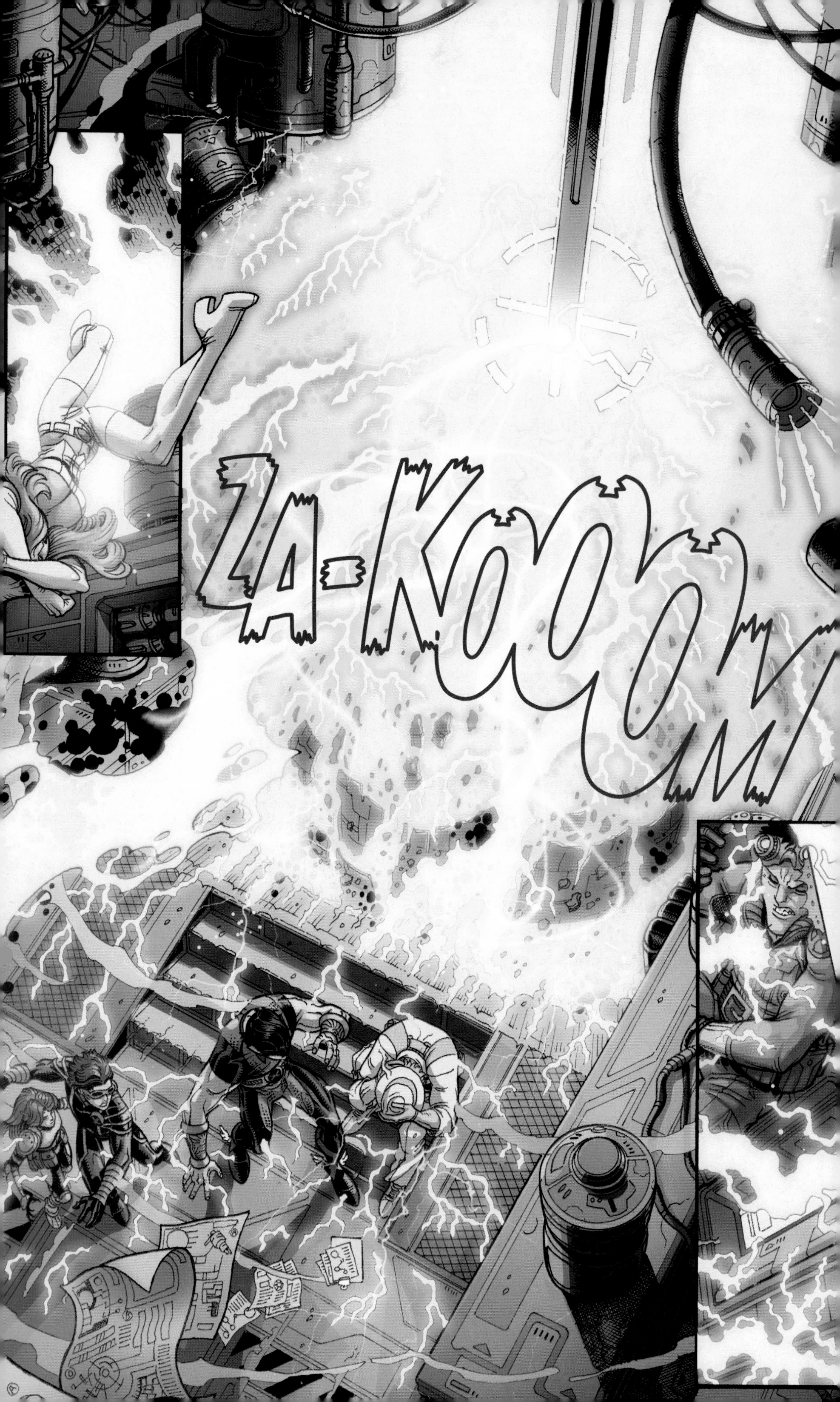
ZA-KOOOOM

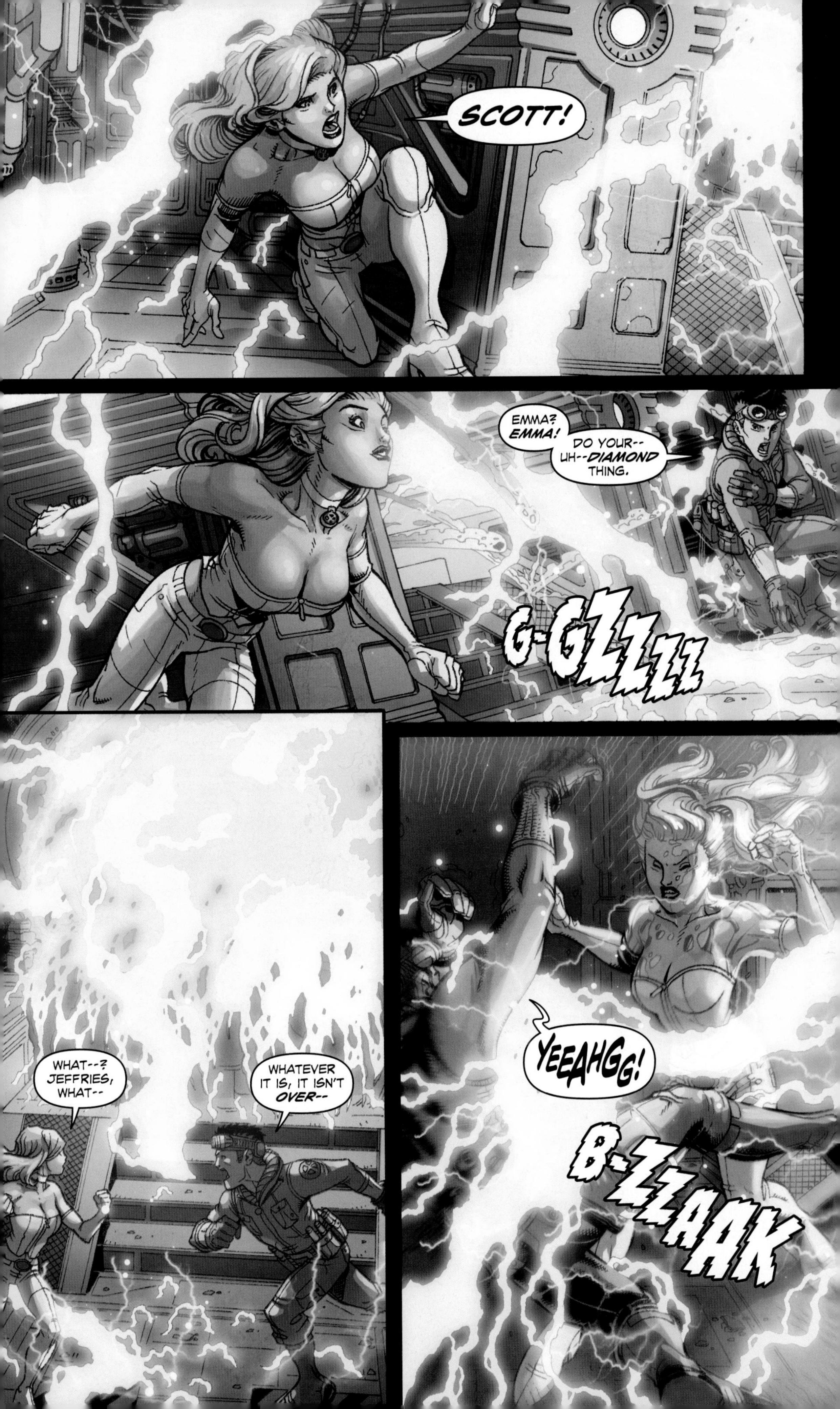
SCOTT!
EMMA? EMMA!
DO YOUR-- UH--DIAMOND THING.
G-GZZZZZ
WHAT--? JEFFRIES, WHAT--
WHATEVER IT IS, IT ISN'T OVER--
YEEAHGG!
B-ZZZAAK

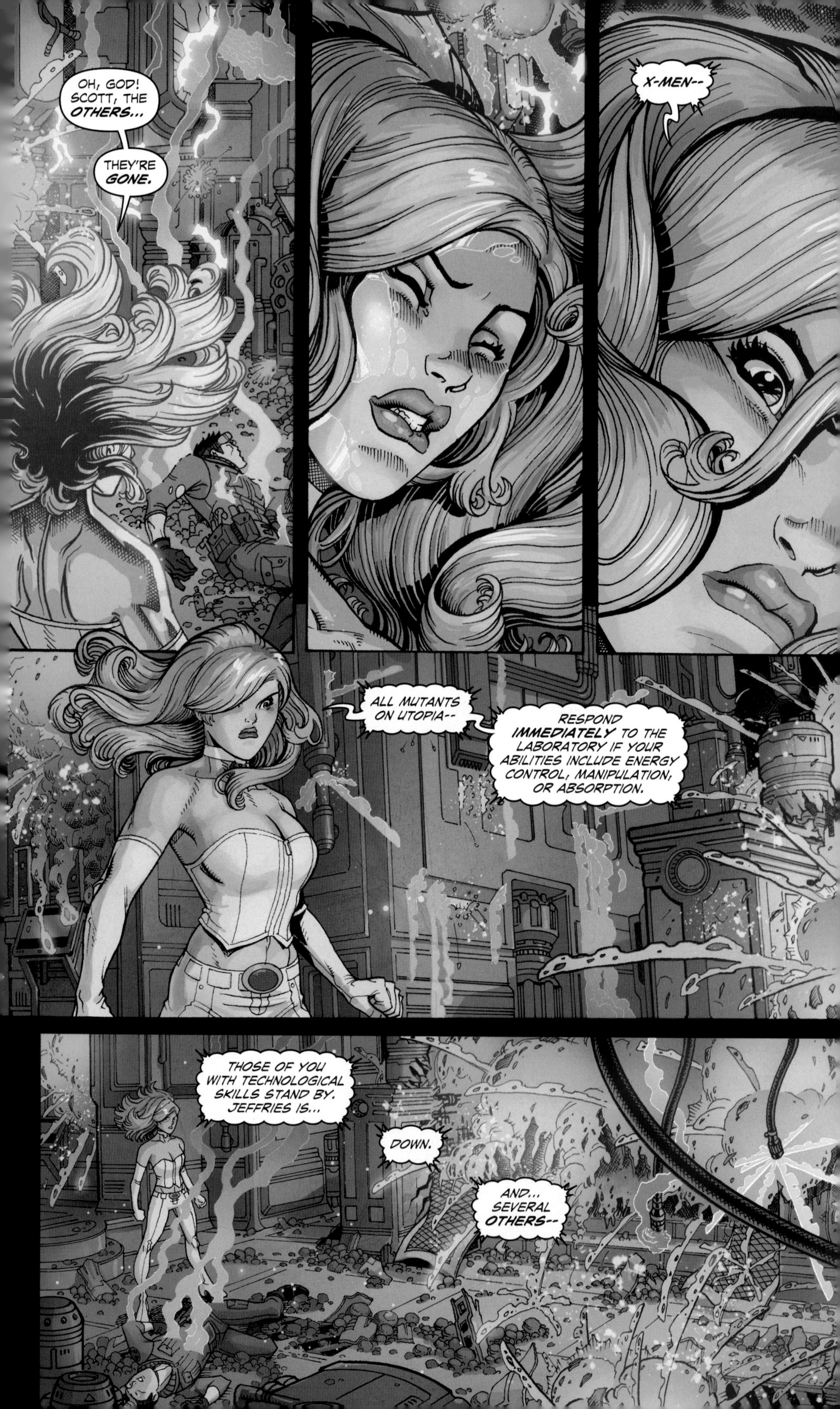
OH, GOD! SCOTT, THE OTHERS...
THEY'RE GONE.
X-MEN--
ALL MUTANTS ON UTOPIA--
RESPOND IMMEDIATELY TO THE LABORATORY IF YOUR ABILITIES INCLUDE ENERGY CONTROL, MANIPULATION, OR ABSORPTION.
THOSE OF YOU WITH TECHNOLOGICAL SKILLS STAND BY. JEFFRIES IS...
DOWN.
AND... SEVERAL OTHERS--

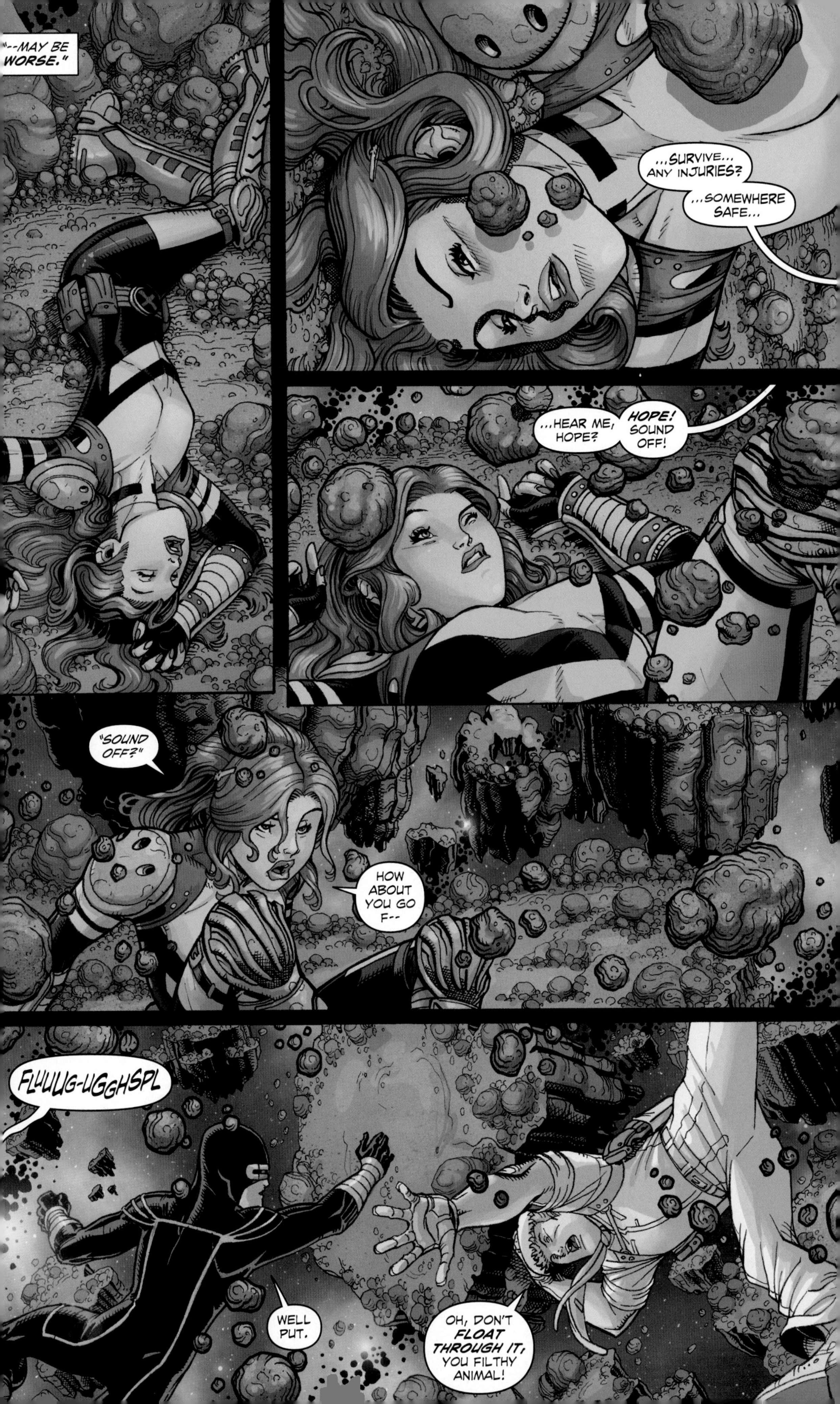
"--MAY BE WORSE."
...SURVIVE... ANY INJURIES?
...SOMEWHERE SAFE...
...HEAR ME, HOPE?
HOPE! SOUND OFF!
"SOUND OFF?"
HOW ABOUT YOU GO F--
FLUUUG-UGGHSPL
WELL PUT.
OH, DON'T FLOAT THROUGH IT, YOU FILTHY ANIMAL!

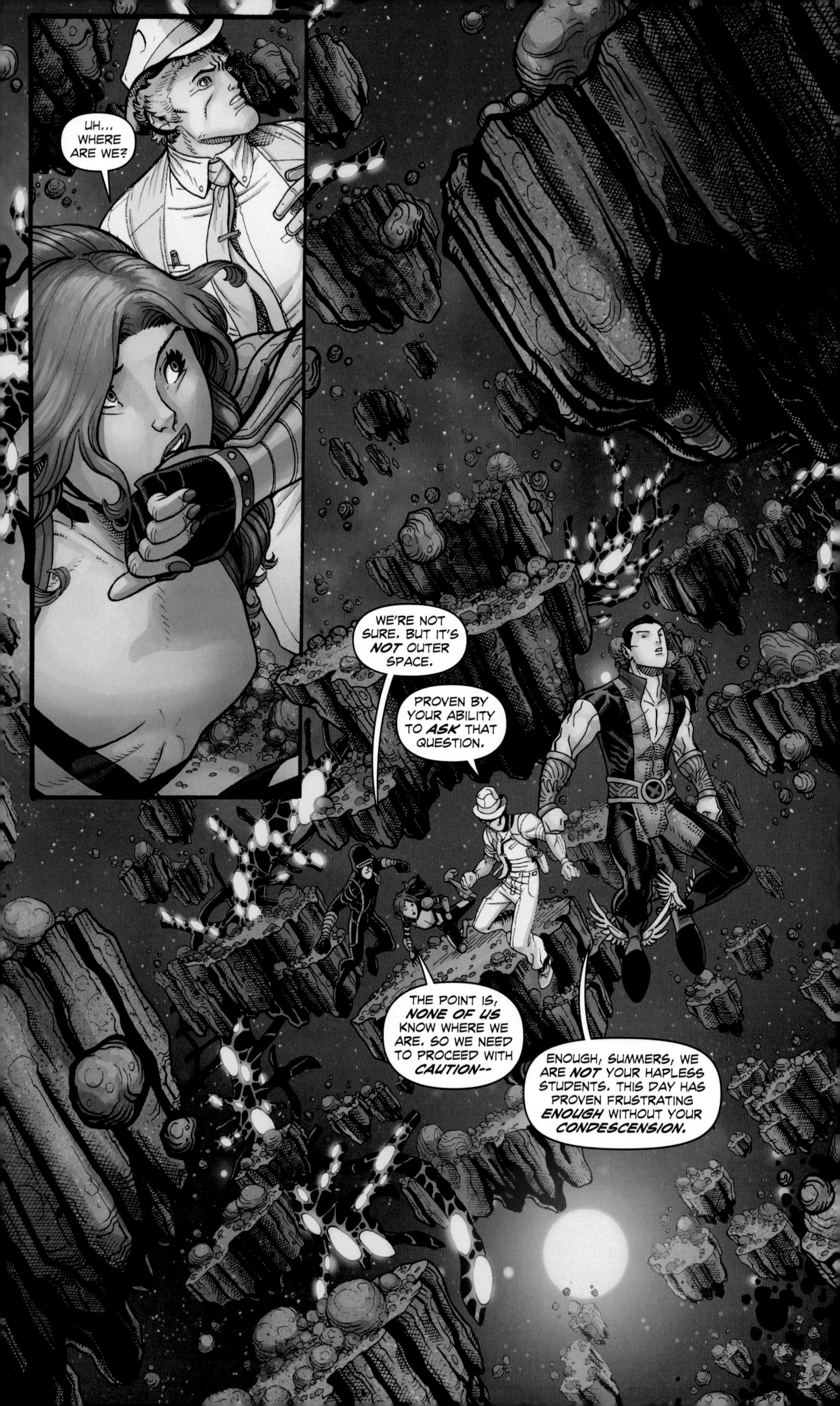
UH... WHERE ARE WE?
WE'RE NOT SURE. BUT IT'S NOT OUTER SPACE.
PROVEN BY YOUR ABILITY TO ASK THAT QUESTION.
THE POINT IS, NONE OF US KNOW WHERE WE ARE. SO WE NEED TO PROCEED WITH CAUTION--
ENOUGH, SUMMERS, WE ARE NOT YOUR HAPLESS STUDENTS. THIS DAY HAS PROVEN FRUSTRATING ENOUGH WITHOUT YOUR CONDESCENSION.

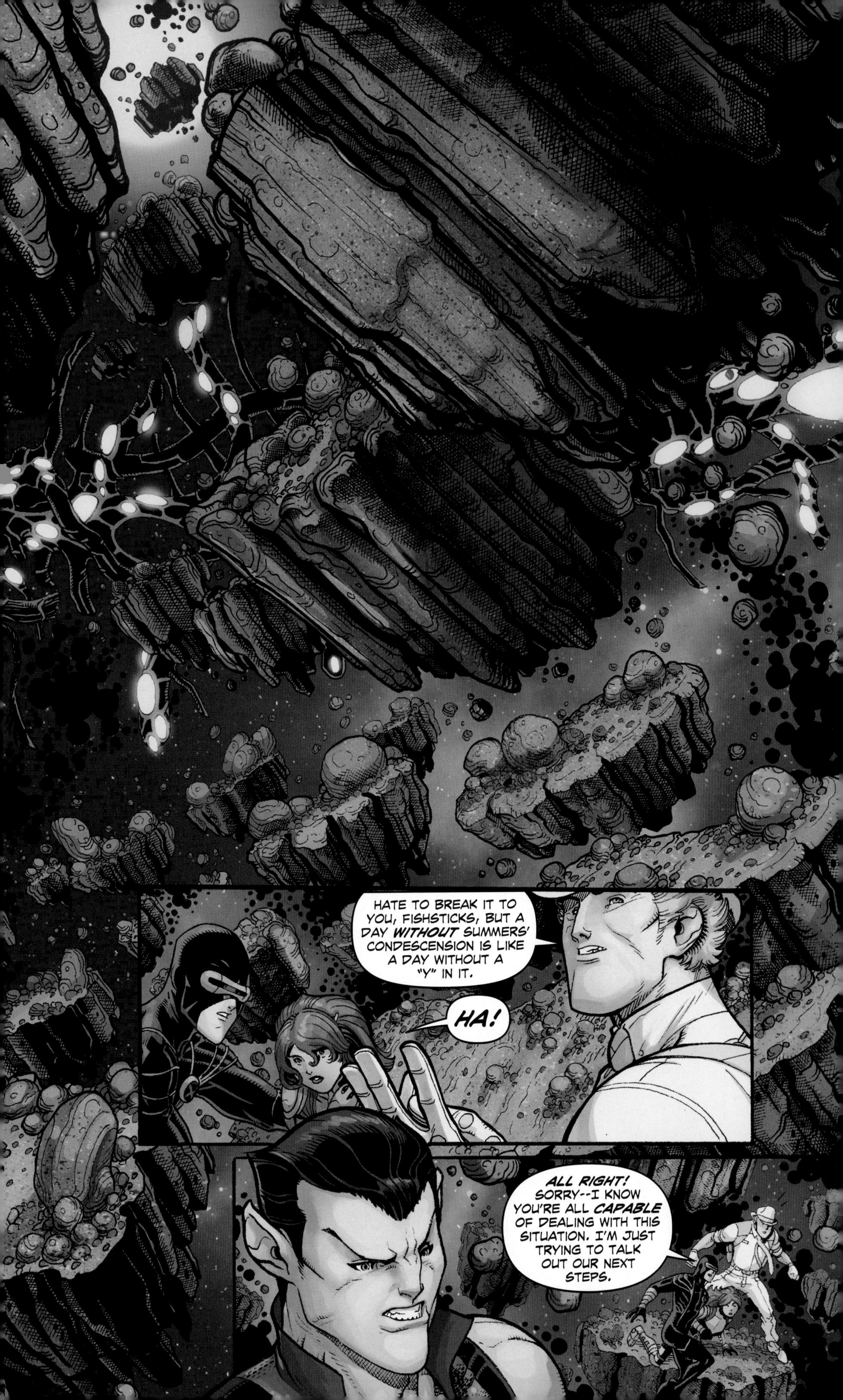
HATE TO BREAK IT TO YOU, FISHSTICKS, BUT A DAY WITHOUT SUMMERS' CONDESCENSION IS LIKE A DAY WITHOUT A "Y" IN IT.
HA!
ALL RIGHT! SORRY--I KNOW YOU'RE ALL CAPABLE OF DEALING WITH THIS SITUATION. I'M JUST TRYING TO TALK OUT OUR NEXT STEPS.

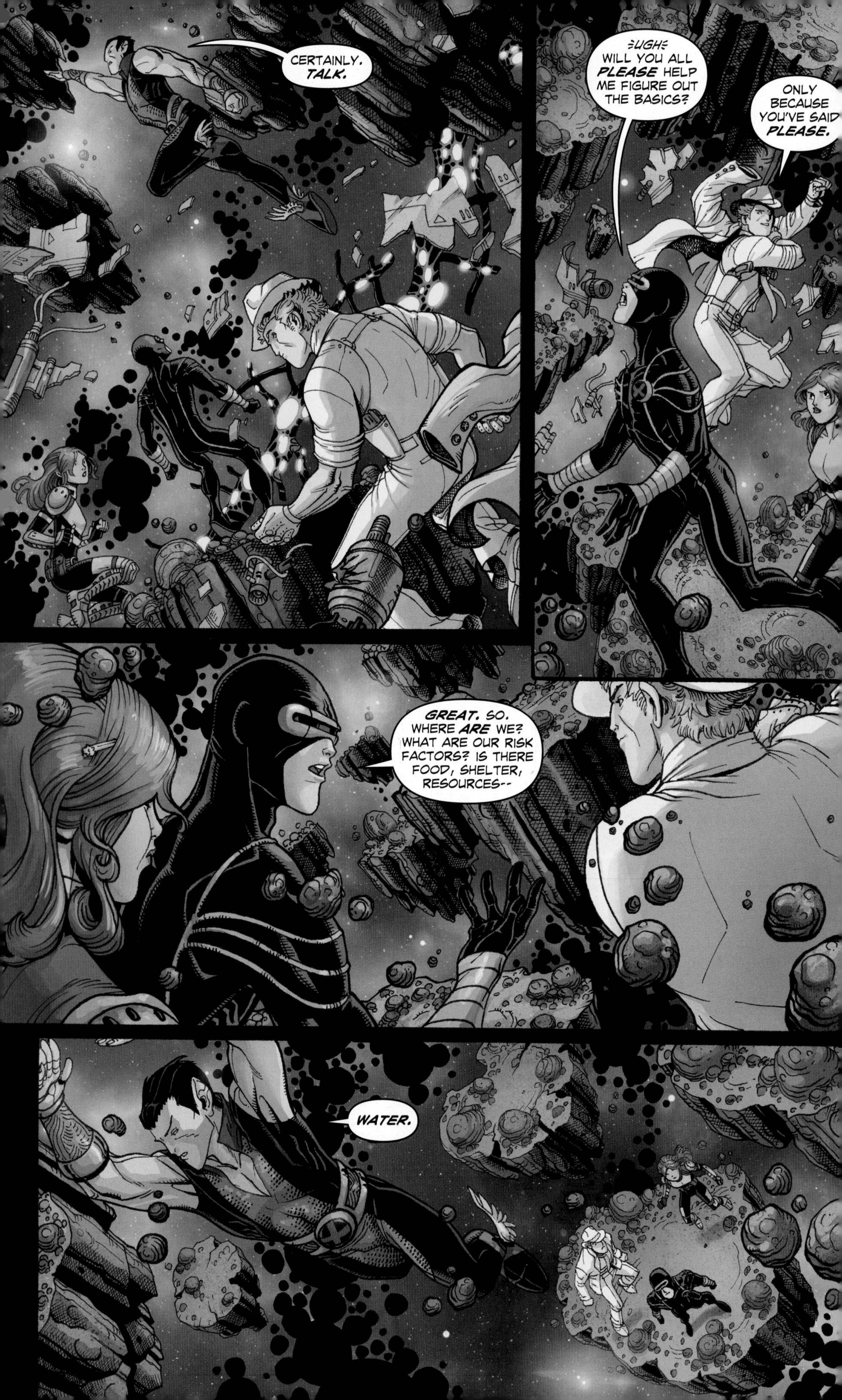
CERTAINLY. TALK.
UGH WILL YOU ALL PLEASE HELP ME FIGURE OUT THE BASICS?
ONLY BECAUSE YOU'VE SAID PLEASE.
GREAT. SO. WHERE ARE WE? WHAT ARE OUR RISK FACTORS? IS THERE FOOD, SHELTER, RESOURCES--
WATER.

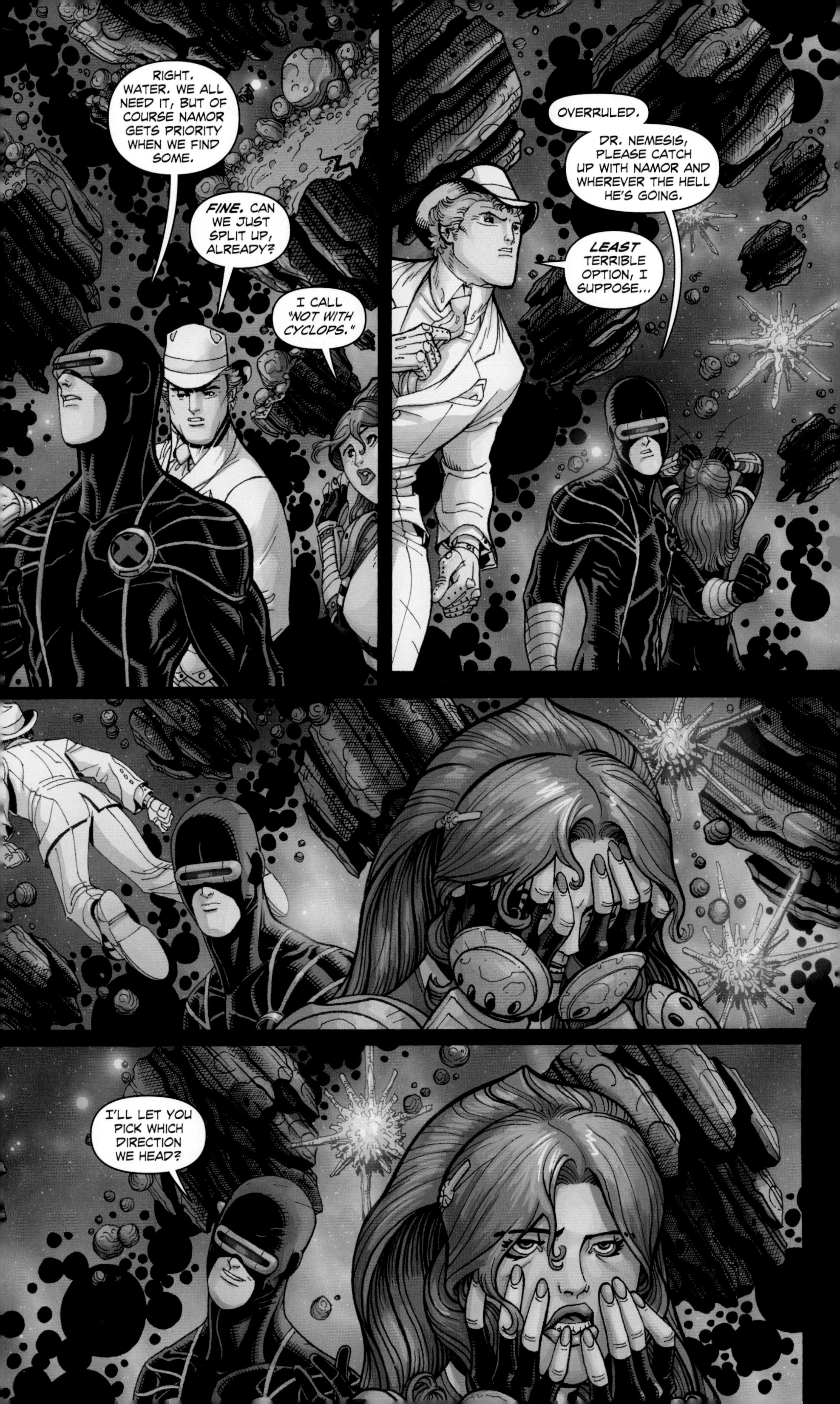
RIGHT. WATER. WE ALL NEED IT, BUT OF COURSE NAMOR GETS PRIORITY WHEN WE FIND SOME.
FINE. CAN WE JUST SPLIT UP, ALREADY?
I CALL "NOT WITH CYCLOPS."
OVERRULED.
DR. NEMESIS, PLEASE CATCH UP WITH NAMOR AND WHEREVER THE HELL HE'S GOING.
LEAST TERRIBLE OPTION, I SUPPOSE...
I'LL LET YOU PICK WHICH DIRECTION WE HEAD?

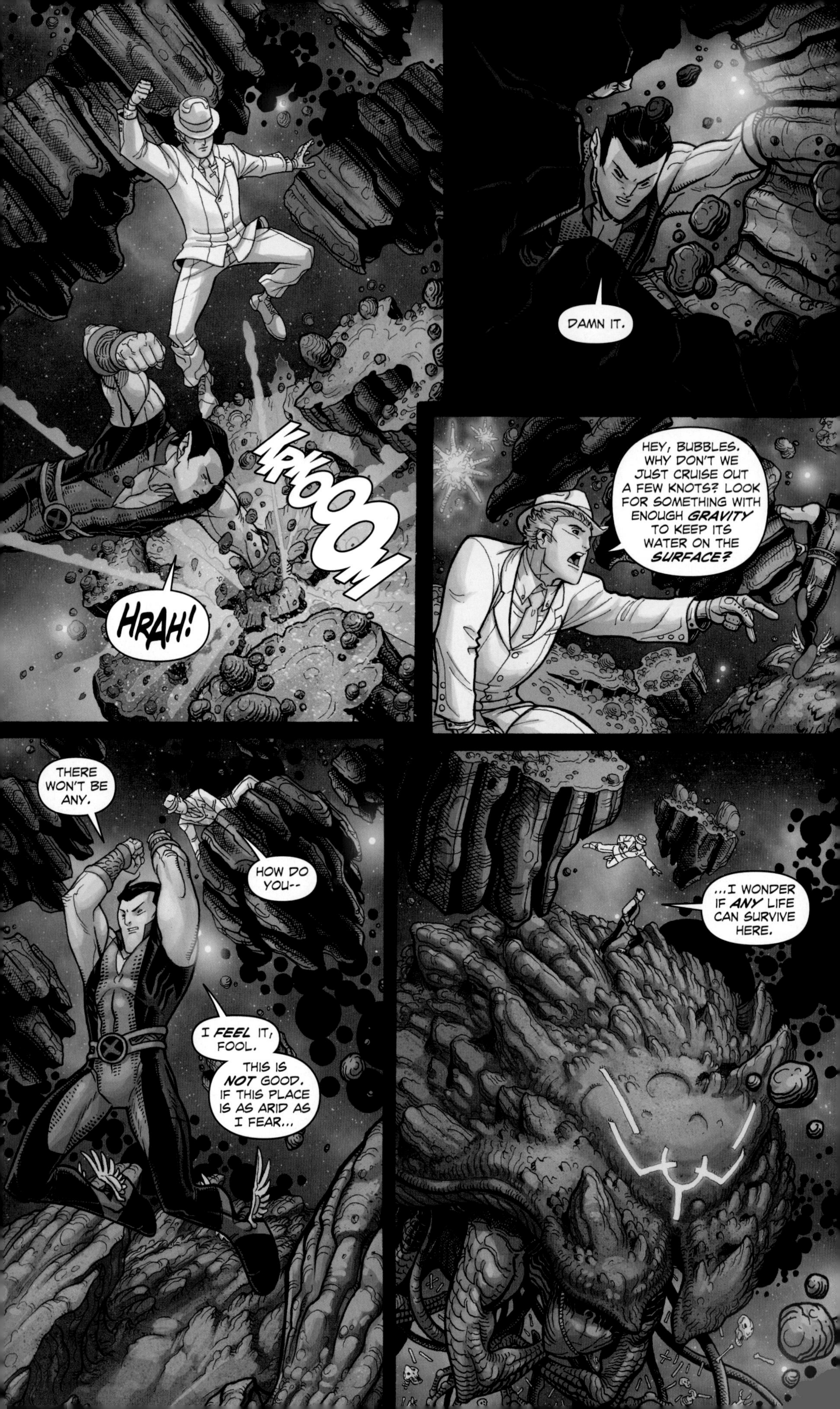
KRKOOOM
HRAH!
DAMN IT.
HEY, BUBBLES. WHY DON'T WE JUST CRUISE OUT A FEW KNOTS? LOOK FOR SOMETHING WITH ENOUGH GRAVITY TO KEEP ITS WATER ON THE SURFACE?
THERE WON'T BE ANY.
HOW DO YOU--
I FEEL IT, FOOL.
THIS IS NOT GOOD. IF THIS PLACE IS AS ARID AS I FEAR...
...I WONDER IF ANY LIFE CAN SURVIVE HERE.

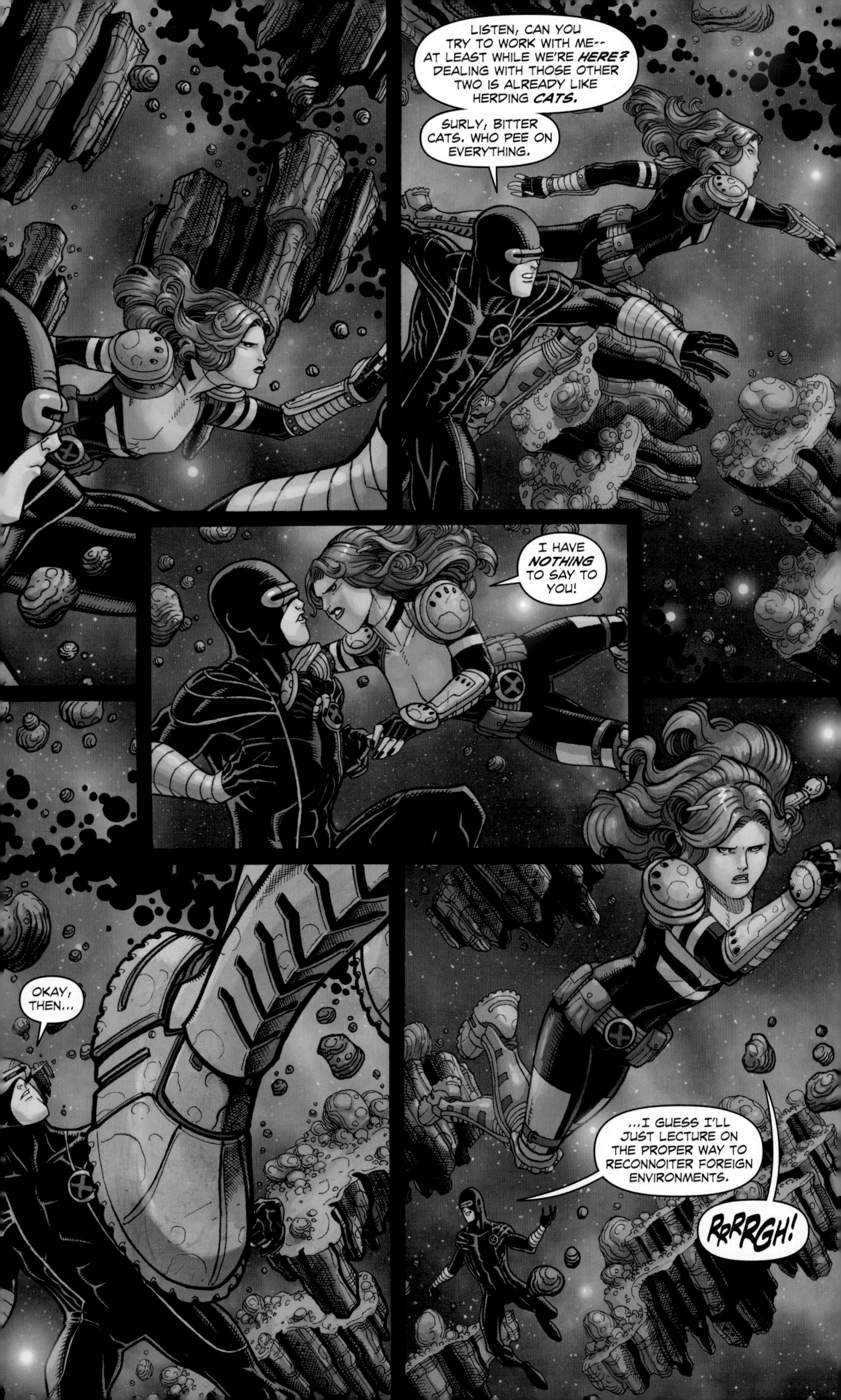

LISTEN, CAN YOU TRY TO WORK WITH ME--AT LEAST WHILE WE'RE HERE? DEALING WITH THOSE OTHER TWO IS ALREADY LIKE HERDING CATS.
SURLY, BITTER CATS. WHO PEE ON EVERYTHING.
I HAVE NOTHING TO SAY TO YOU!
OKAY, THEN...
...I GUESS I'LL JUST LECTURE ON THE PROPER WAY TO RECONNOITER FOREIGN ENVIRONMENTS.
RRRRGH!

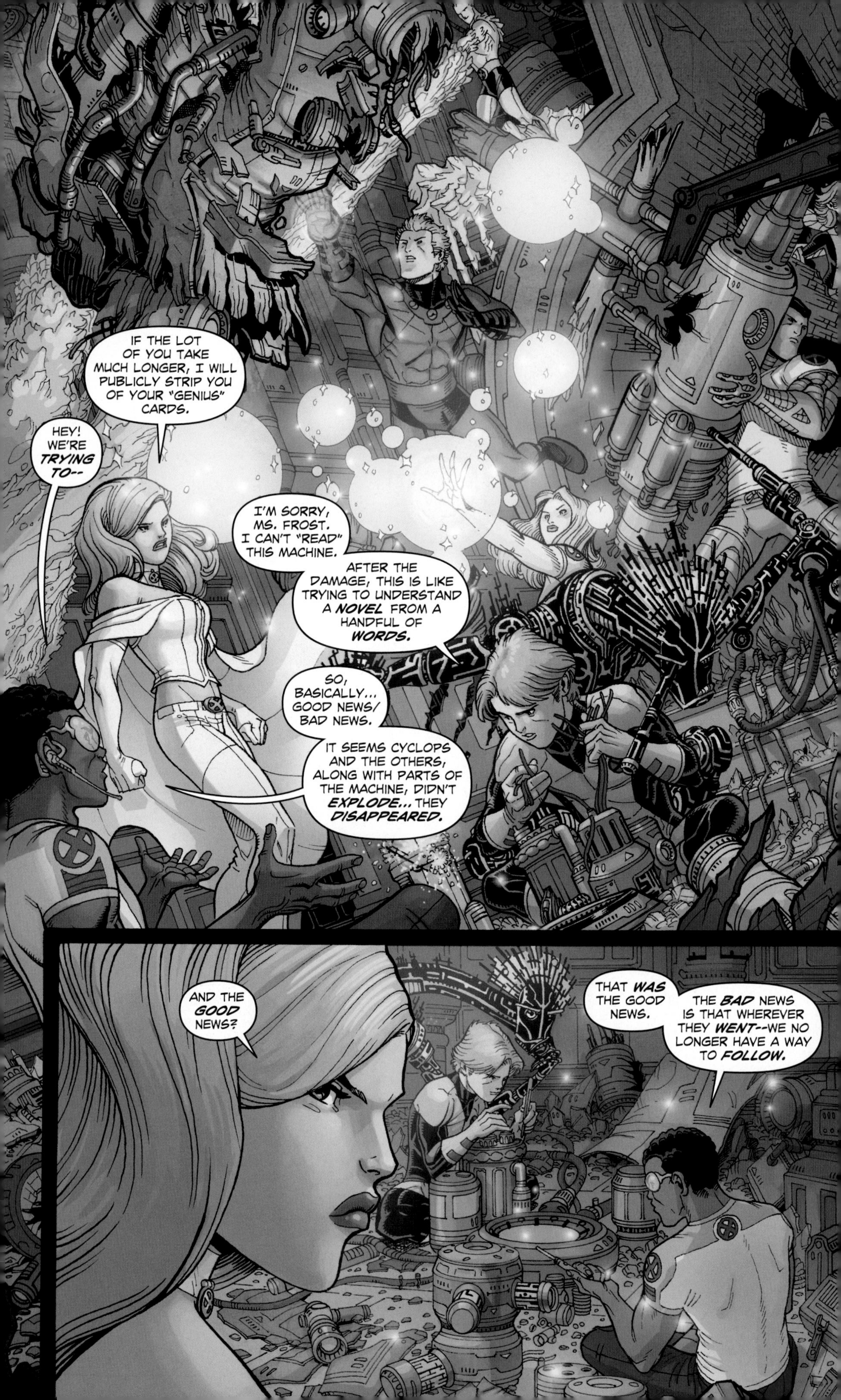

IF THE LOT OF YOU TAKE MUCH LONGER, I WILL PUBLICLY STRIP YOU OF YOUR "GENIUS" CARDS.
HEY! WE'RE TRYING TO--
I'M SORRY, MS. FROST. I CAN'T "READ" THIS MACHINE.
AFTER THE DAMAGE, THIS IS LIKE TRYING TO UNDERSTAND A NOVEL FROM A HANDFUL OF WORDS.
SO, BASICALLY... GOOD NEWS/ BAD NEWS.
IT SEEMS CYCLOPS AND THE OTHERS, ALONG WITH PARTS OF THE MACHINE, DIDN'T EXPLODE... THEY DISAPPEARED.
AND THE GOOD NEWS?
THAT WAS THE GOOD NEWS.
THE BAD NEWS IS THAT WHEREVER THEY WENT--WE NO LONGER HAVE A WAY TO FOLLOW.

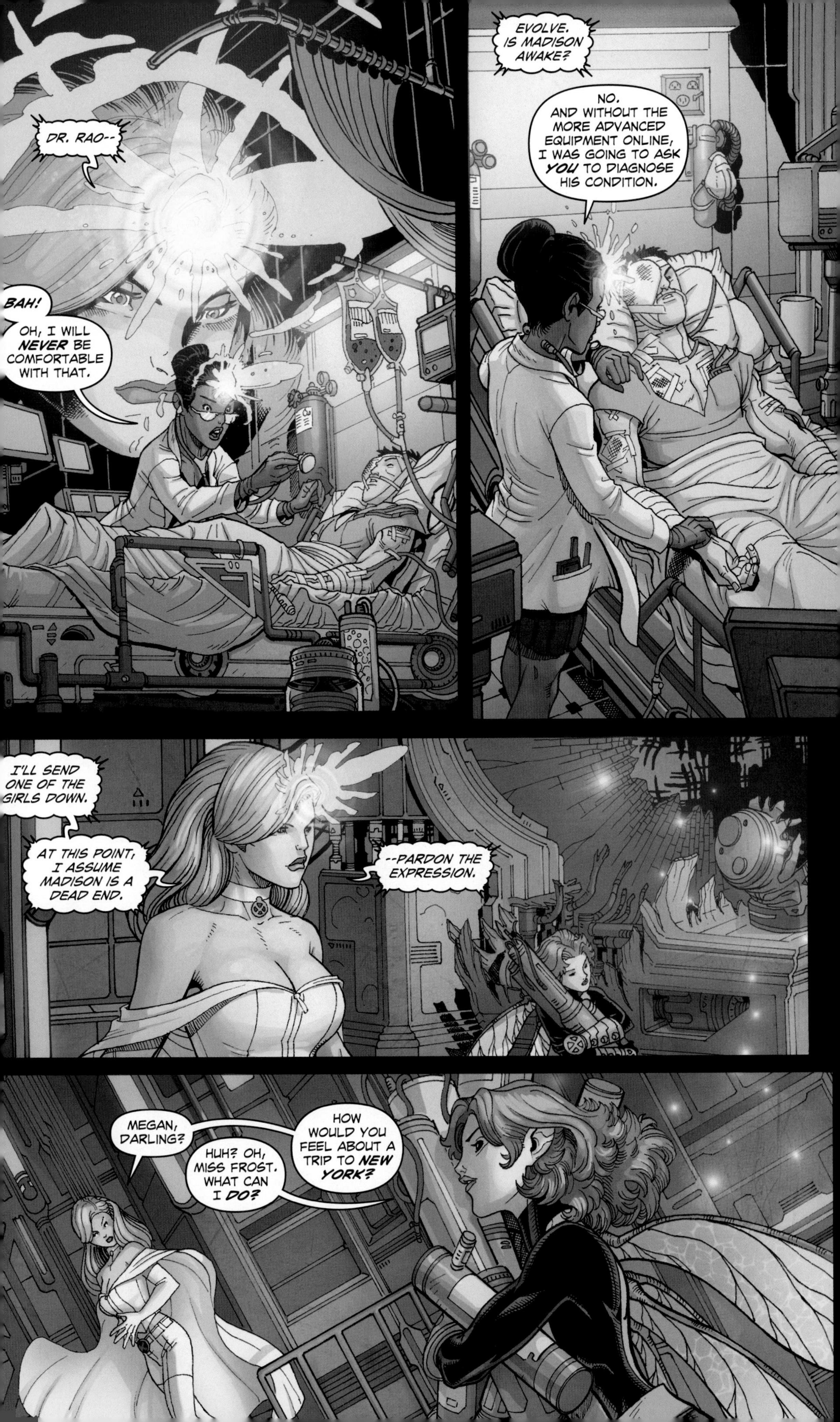
DR. RAO--
BAH!
OH, I WILL NEVER BE COMFORTABLE WITH THAT.
EVOLVE. IS MADISON AWAKE?
NO. AND WITHOUT THE MORE ADVANCED EQUIPMENT ONLINE, I WAS GOING TO ASK YOU TO DIAGNOSE HIS CONDITION.
I'LL SEND ONE OF THE GIRLS DOWN.
AT THIS POINT, I ASSUME MADISON IS A DEAD END.
--PARDON THE EXPRESSION.
MEGAN, DARLING?
HUH? OH, MISS FROST. WHAT CAN I DO?
HOW WOULD YOU FEEL ABOUT A TRIP TO NEW YORK?

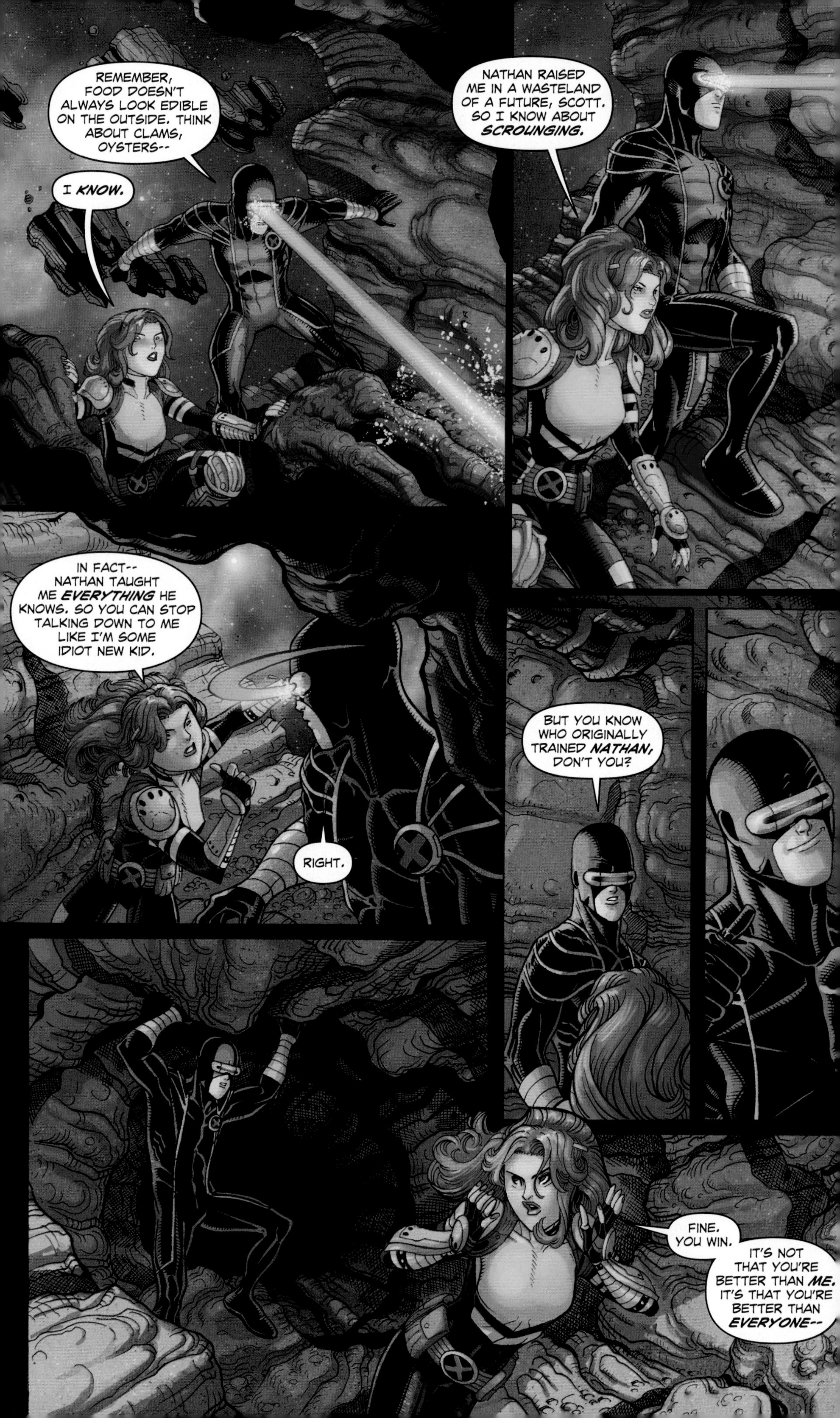
REMEMBER, FOOD DOESN'T ALWAYS LOOK EDIBLE ON THE OUTSIDE. THINK ABOUT CLAMS, OYSTERS--
I KNOW.
NATHAN RAISED ME IN A WASTELAND OF A FUTURE, SCOTT. SO I KNOW ABOUT SCROUNGING.
IN FACT-- NATHAN TAUGHT ME EVERYTHING HE KNOWS. SO YOU CAN STOP TALKING DOWN TO ME LIKE I'M SOME IDIOT NEW KID.
RIGHT.
BUT YOU KNOW WHO ORIGINALLY TRAINED NATHAN, DON'T YOU?
FINE. YOU WIN.
IT'S NOT THAT YOU'RE BETTER THAN ME. IT'S THAT YOU'RE BETTER THAN EVERYONE--

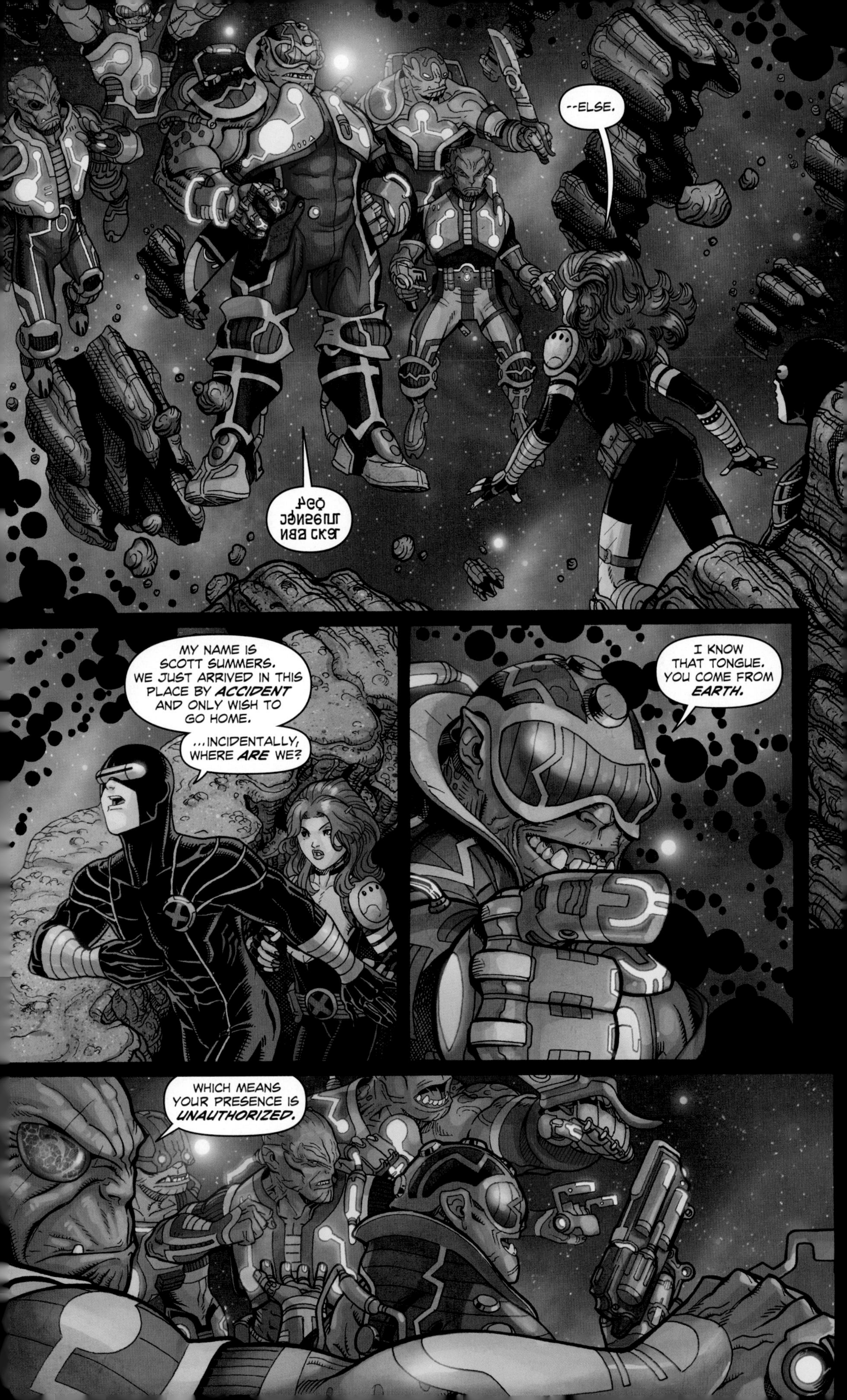
--ELSE.
MY NAME IS SCOTT SUMMERS. WE JUST ARRIVED IN THIS PLACE BY ACCIDENT AND ONLY WISH TO GO HOME.
...INCIDENTALLY, WHERE ARE WE?
I KNOW THAT TONGUE. YOU COME FROM EARTH.
WHICH MEANS YOUR PRESENCE IS UNAUTHORIZED.

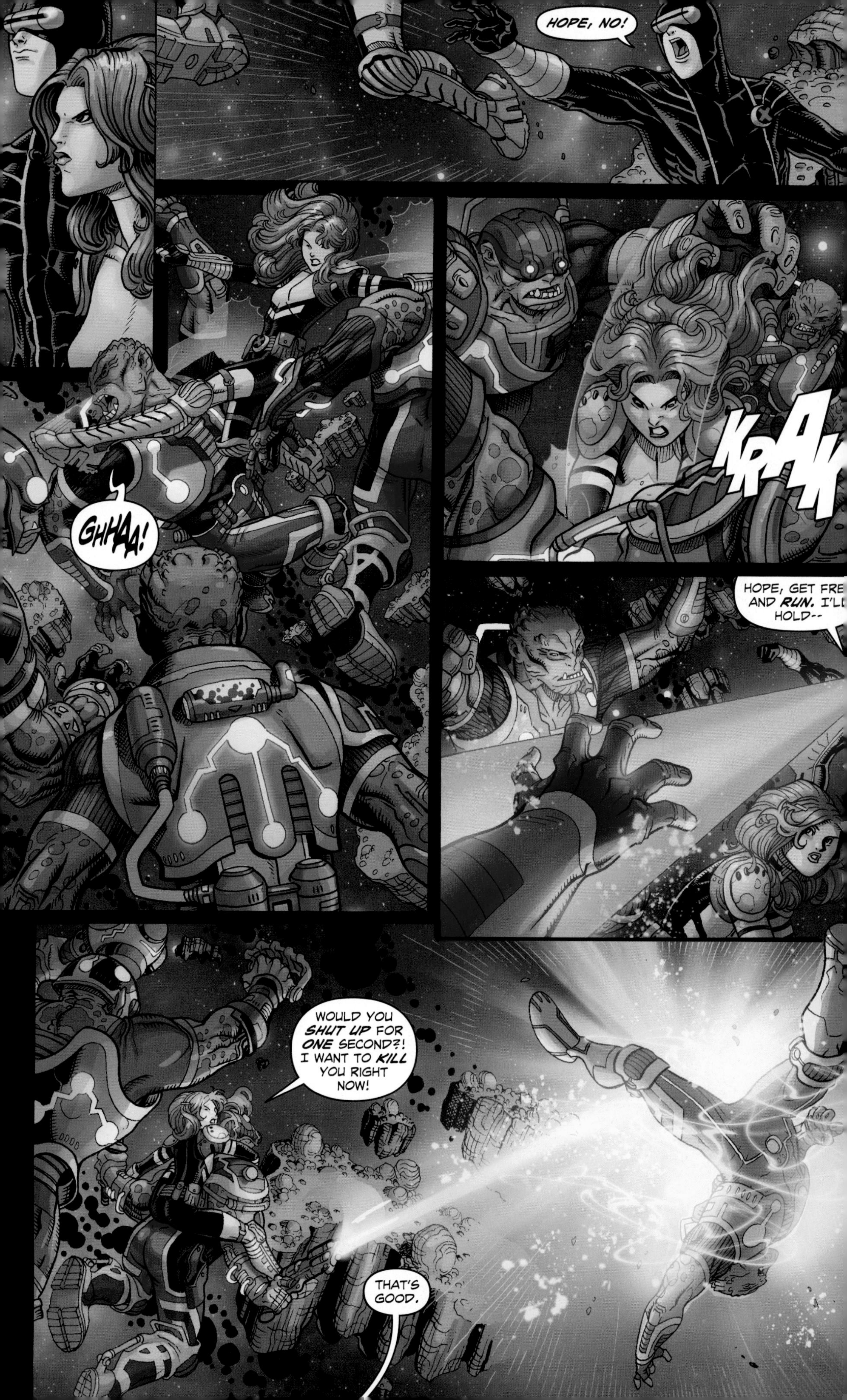

HOPE, NO!
GHHAA!
KRAAK
HOPE, GET FRE
AND RUN. I'LL
HOLD--
WOULD YOU SHUT UP FOR ONE SECOND?! I WANT TO KILL YOU RIGHT NOW!
THAT'S GOOD.

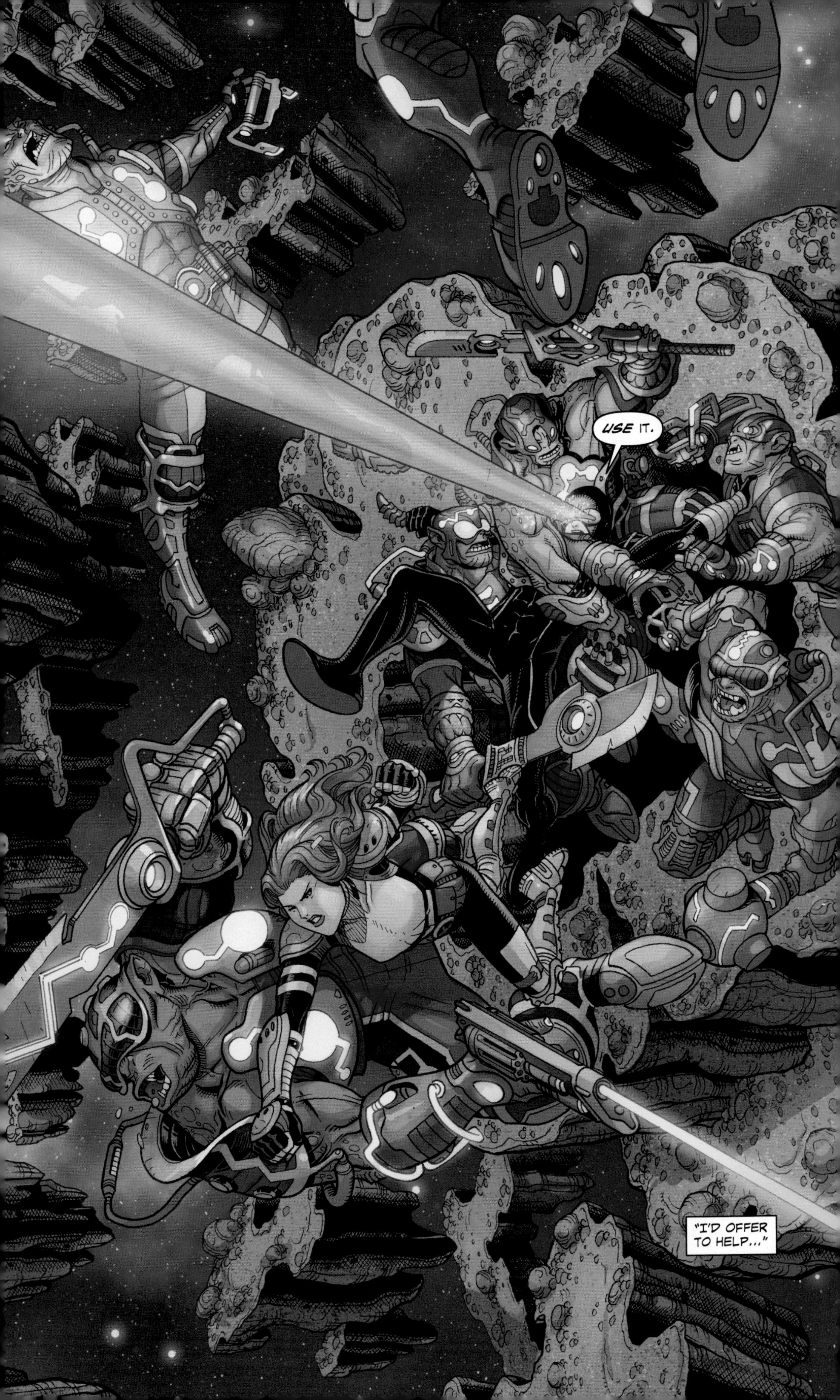

USE IT.
"I'D OFFER TO HELP..."

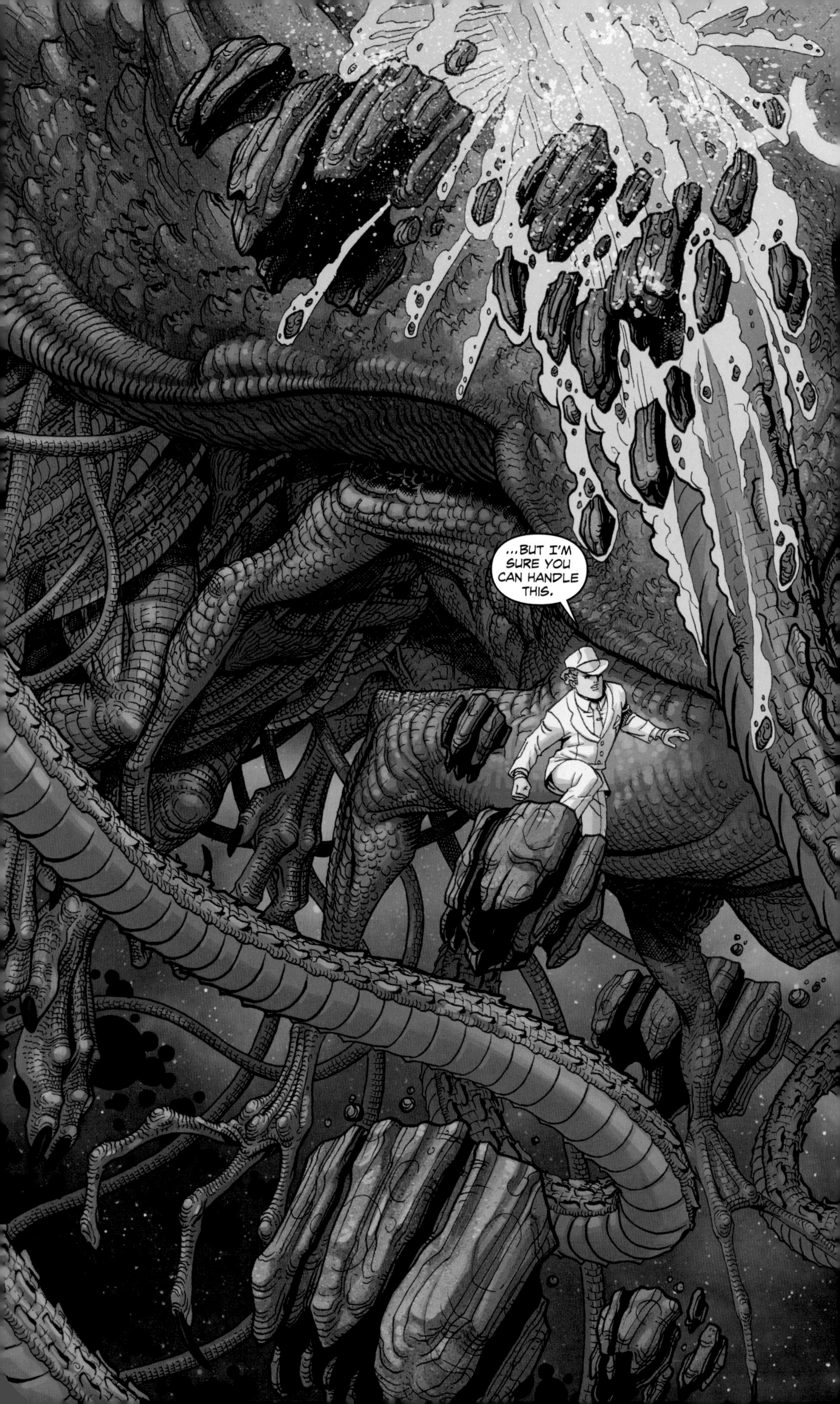
...BUT I'M SURE YOU CAN HANDLE THIS.

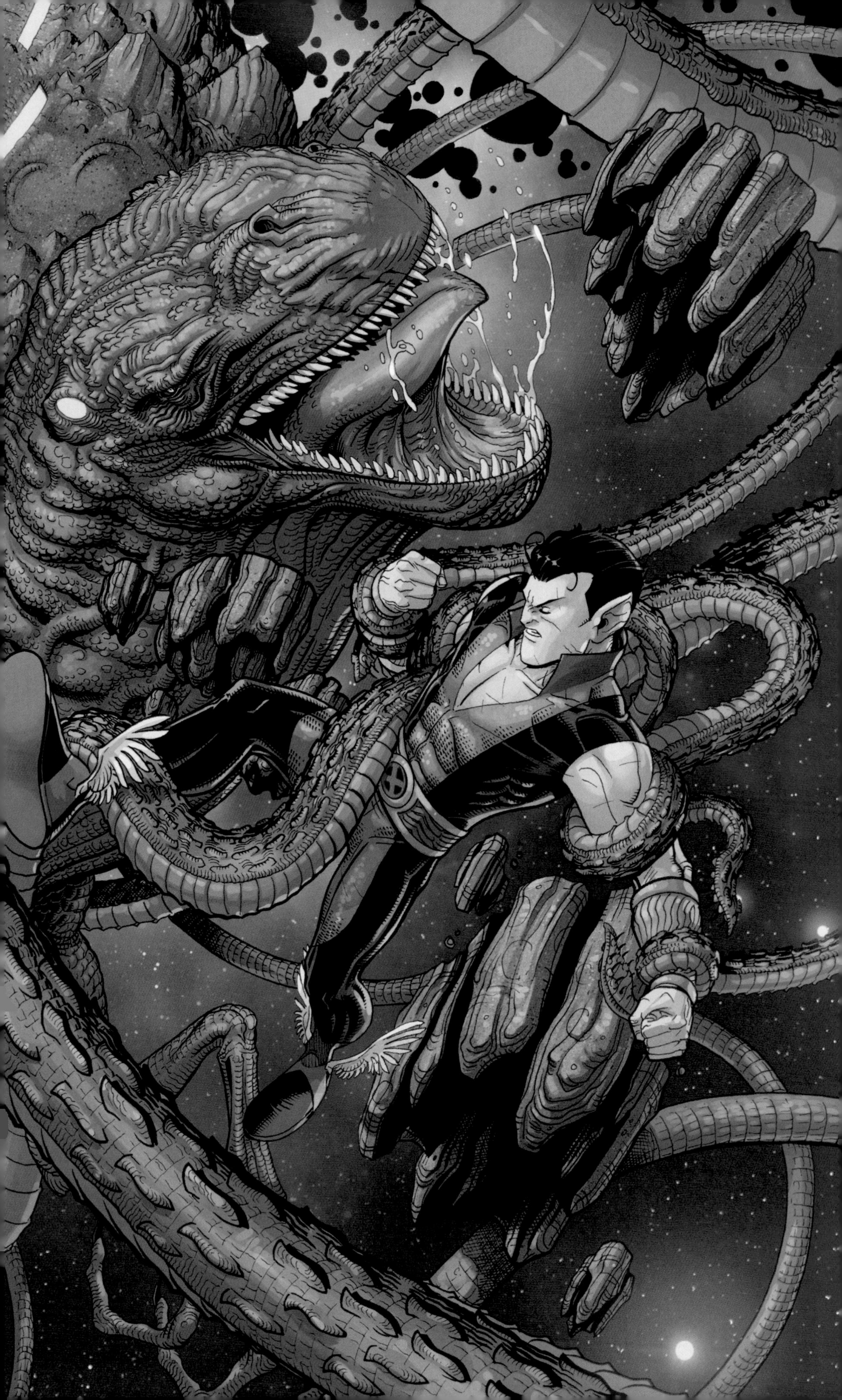

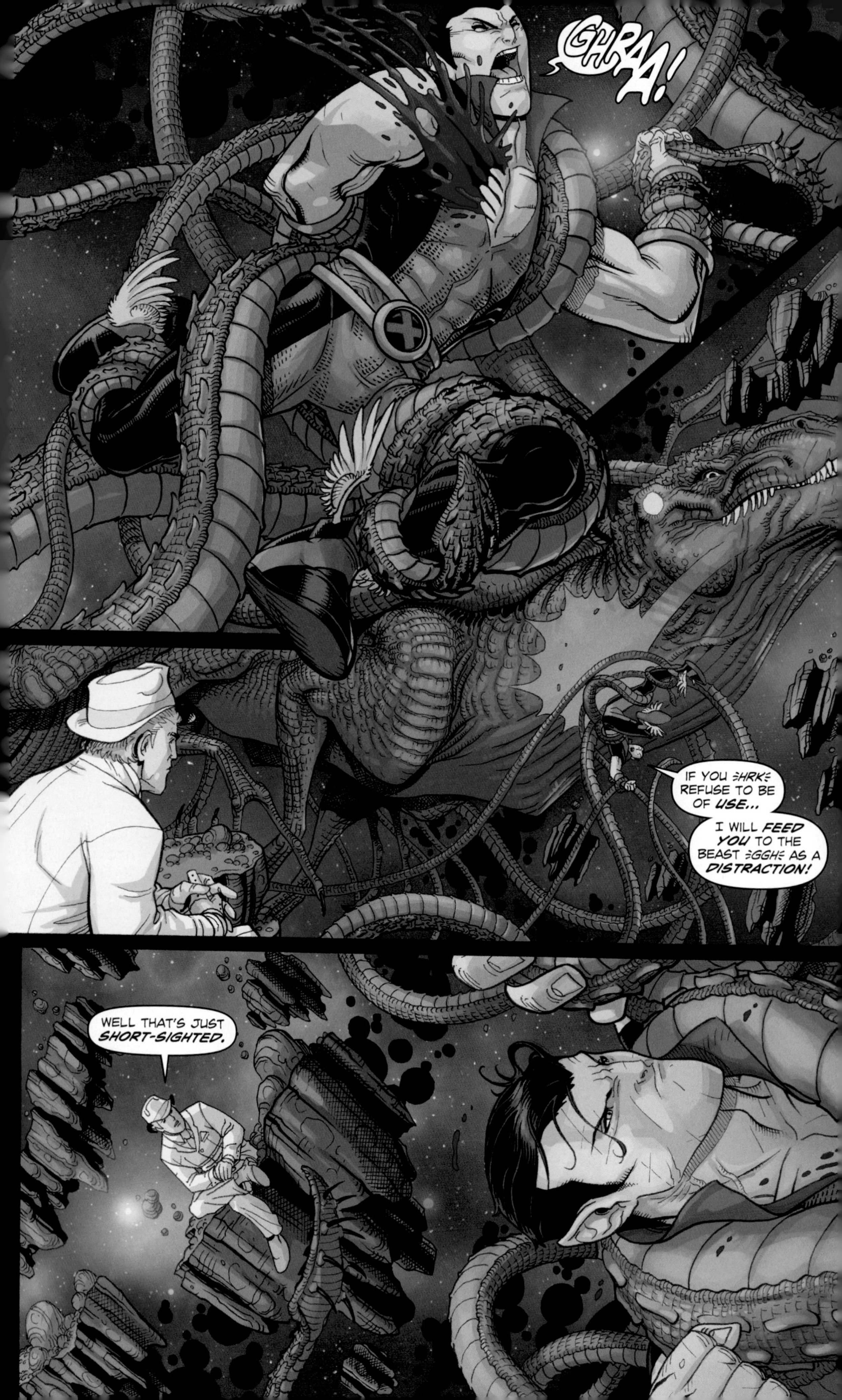

GHRAAA!
IF YOU ≡HRK≡ REFUSE TO BE OF USE...
I WILL FEED YOU TO THE BEAST ≡GGH≡ AS A DISTRACTION!
WELL THAT'S JUST SHORT-SIGHTED.

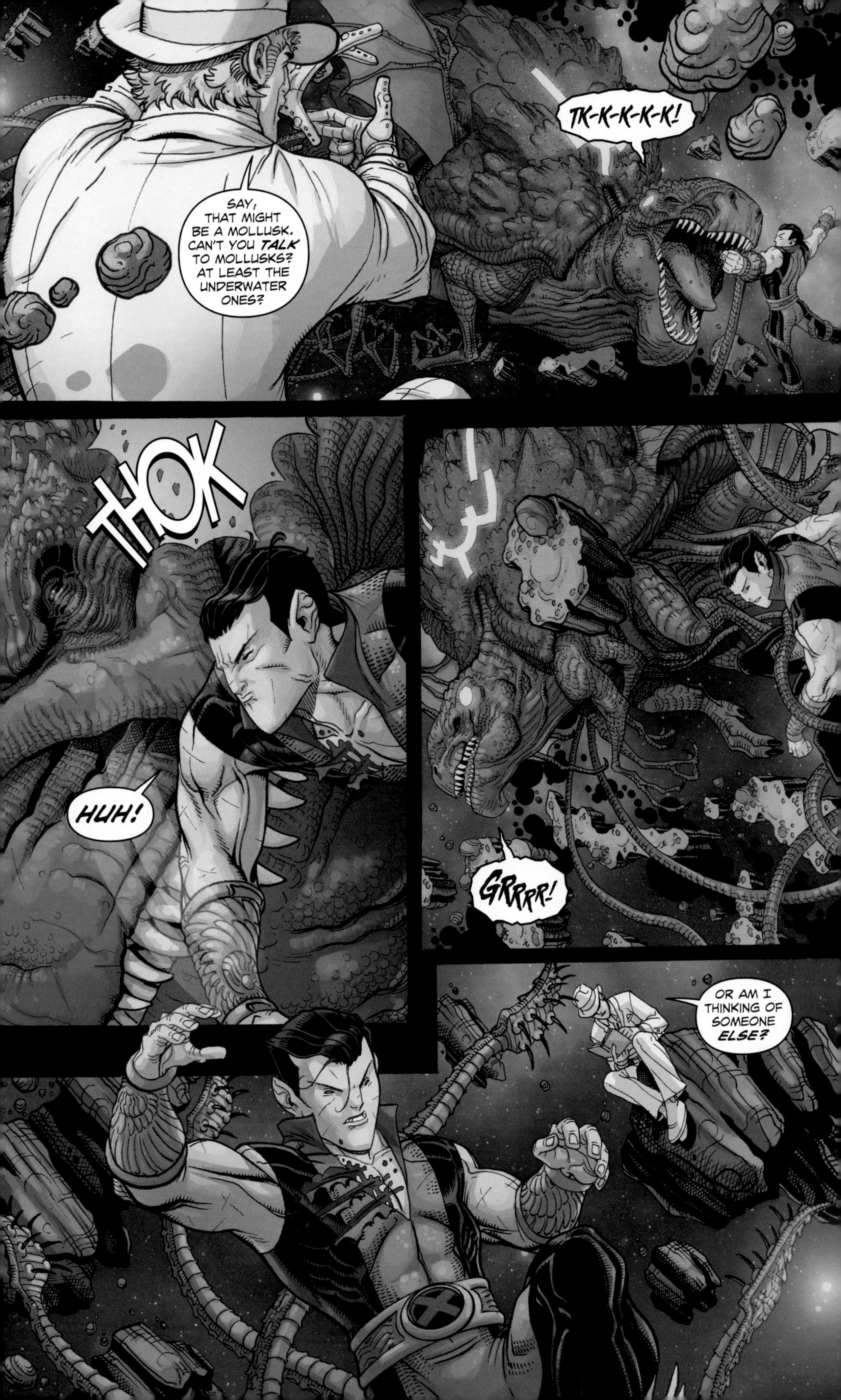
TK-K-K-K-K!
SAY, THAT MIGHT BE A MOLLUSK. CAN'T YOU *TALK* TO MOLLUSKS? AT LEAST THE UNDERWATER ONES?
THOK
HUH!
GRRRR!
OR AM I THINKING OF SOMEONE *ELSE?*

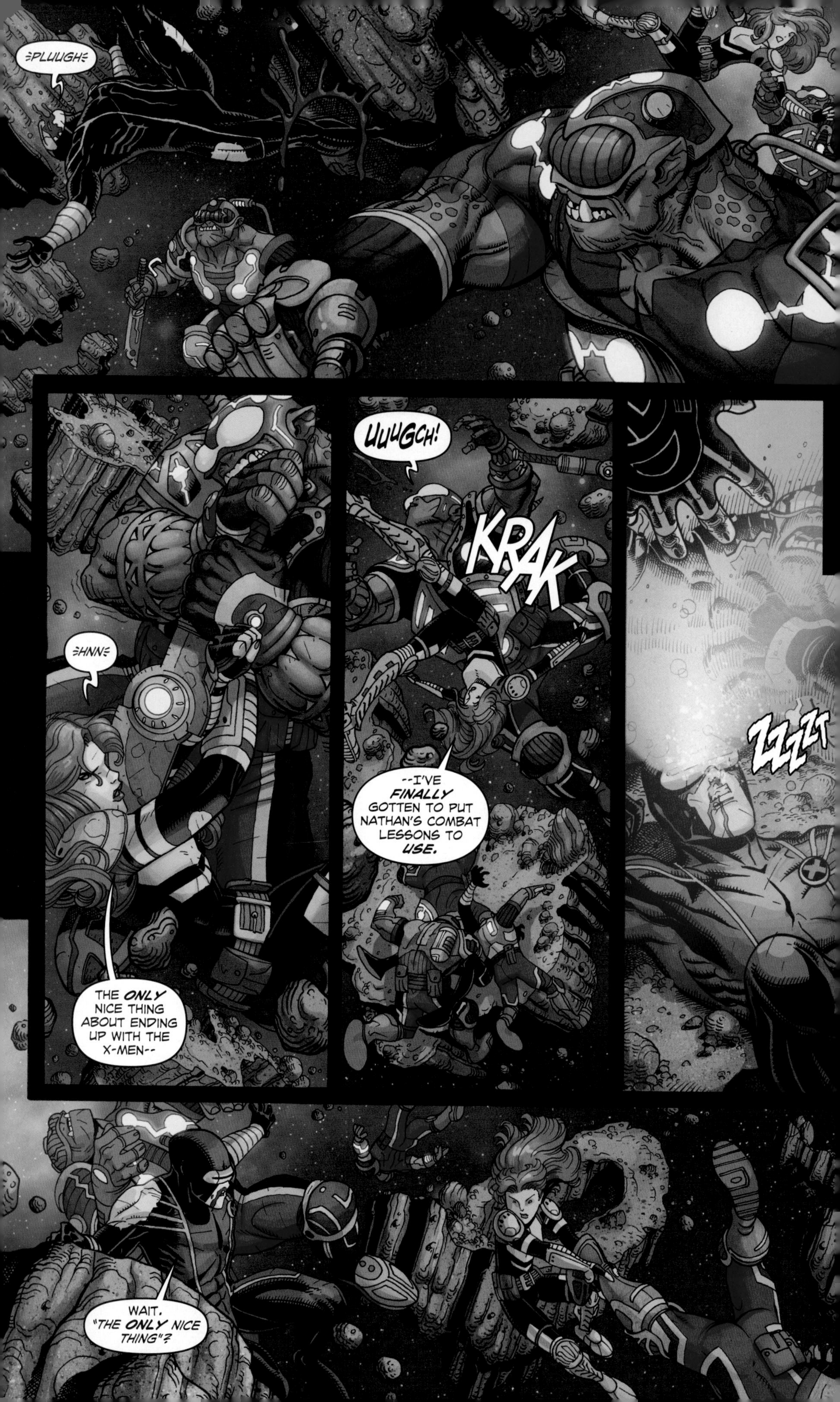
PLUUGH
HNN
THE ONLY NICE THING ABOUT ENDING UP WITH THE X-MEN--
UUUGCH!
KRAK
--I'VE FINALLY GOTTEN TO PUT NATHAN'S COMBAT LESSONS TO USE.
ZZZZT
WAIT. "THE ONLY NICE THING"?

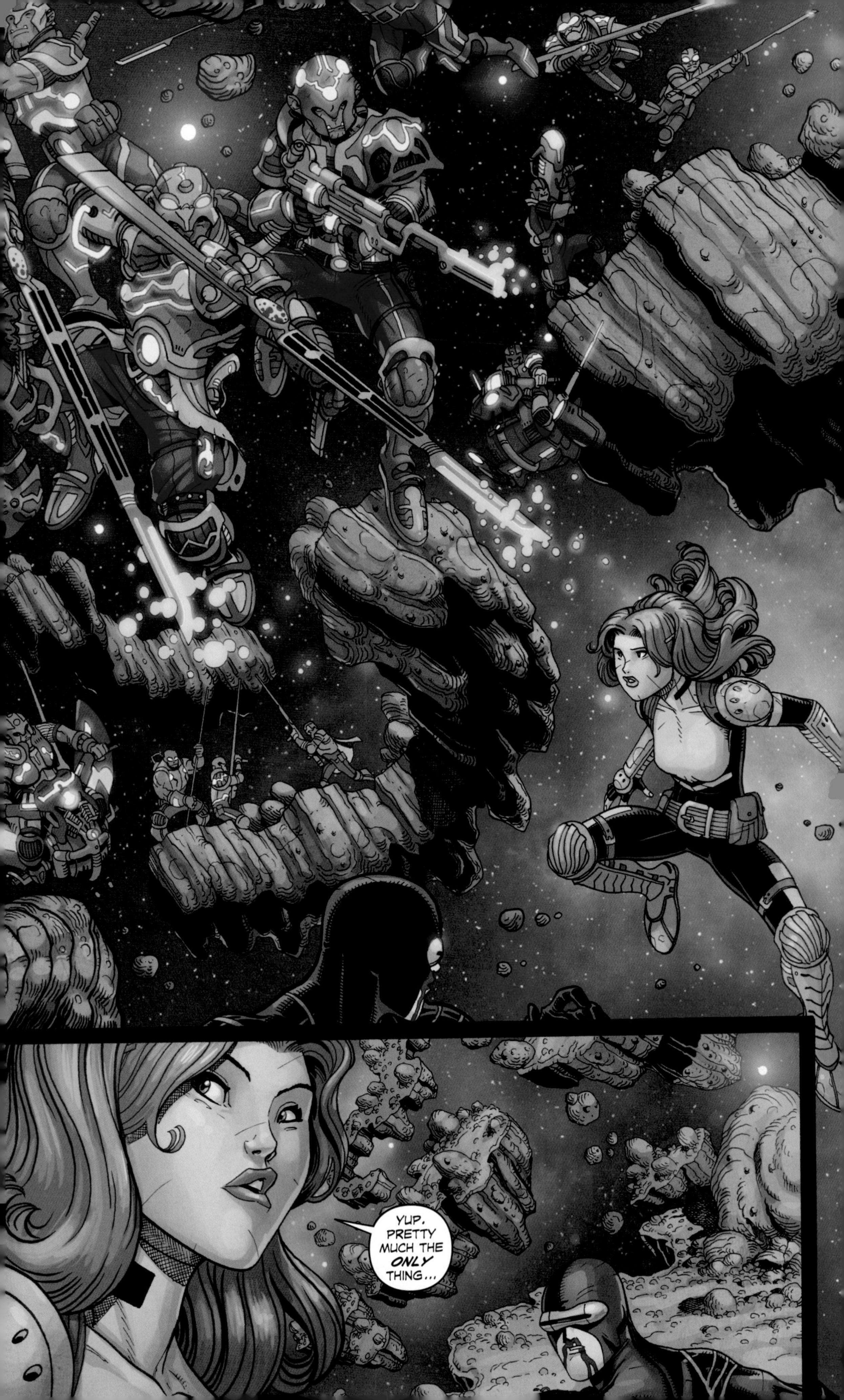
YUP. PRETTY MUCH THE ONLY THING...

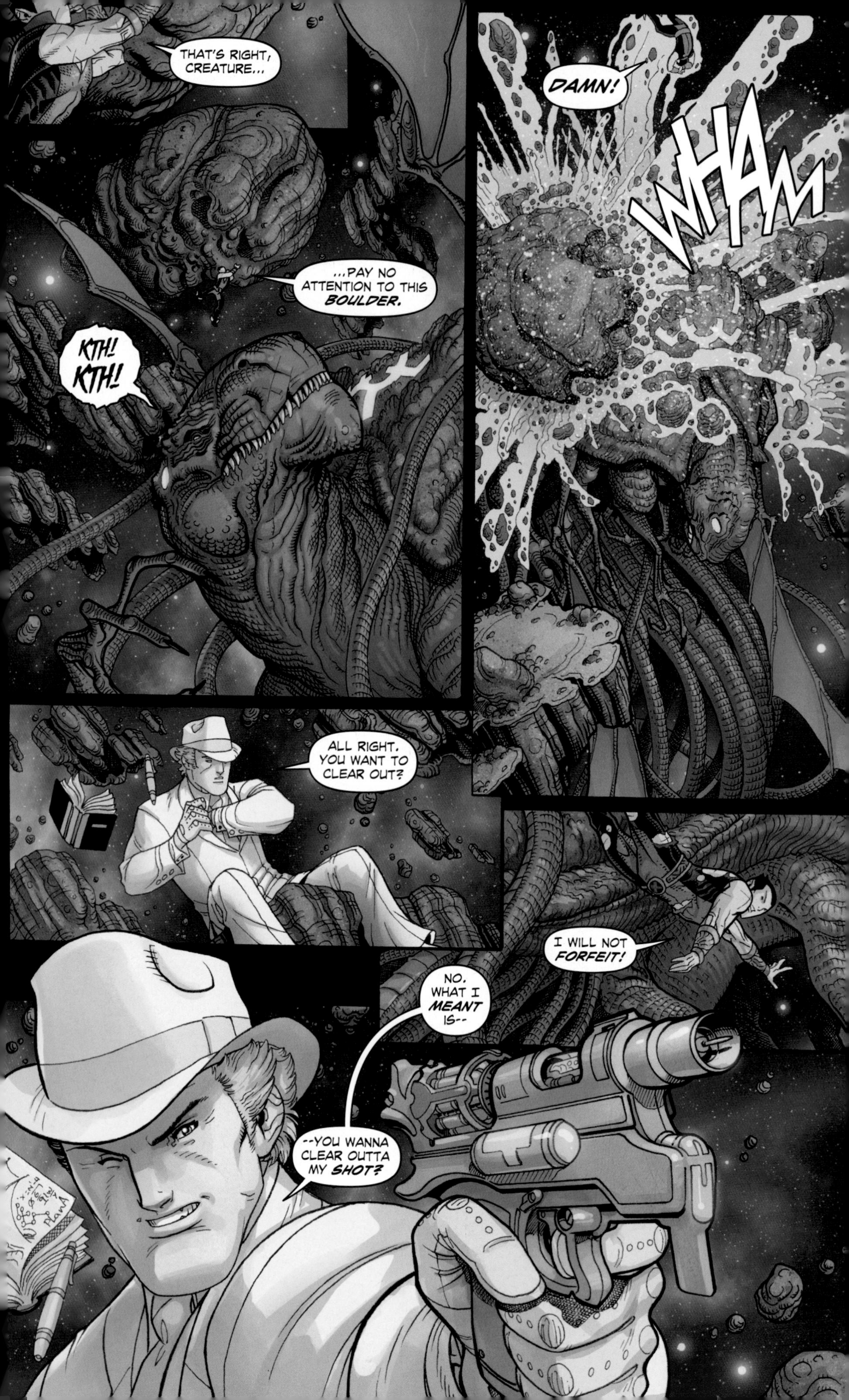
THAT'S RIGHT, CREATURE...
...PAY NO ATTENTION TO THIS BOULDER.
KTH! KTH!
DAMN!
WHAM
ALL RIGHT. YOU WANT TO CLEAR OUT?
I WILL NOT FORFEIT!
NO. WHAT I MEANT IS--
--YOU WANNA CLEAR OUTTA MY SHOT?

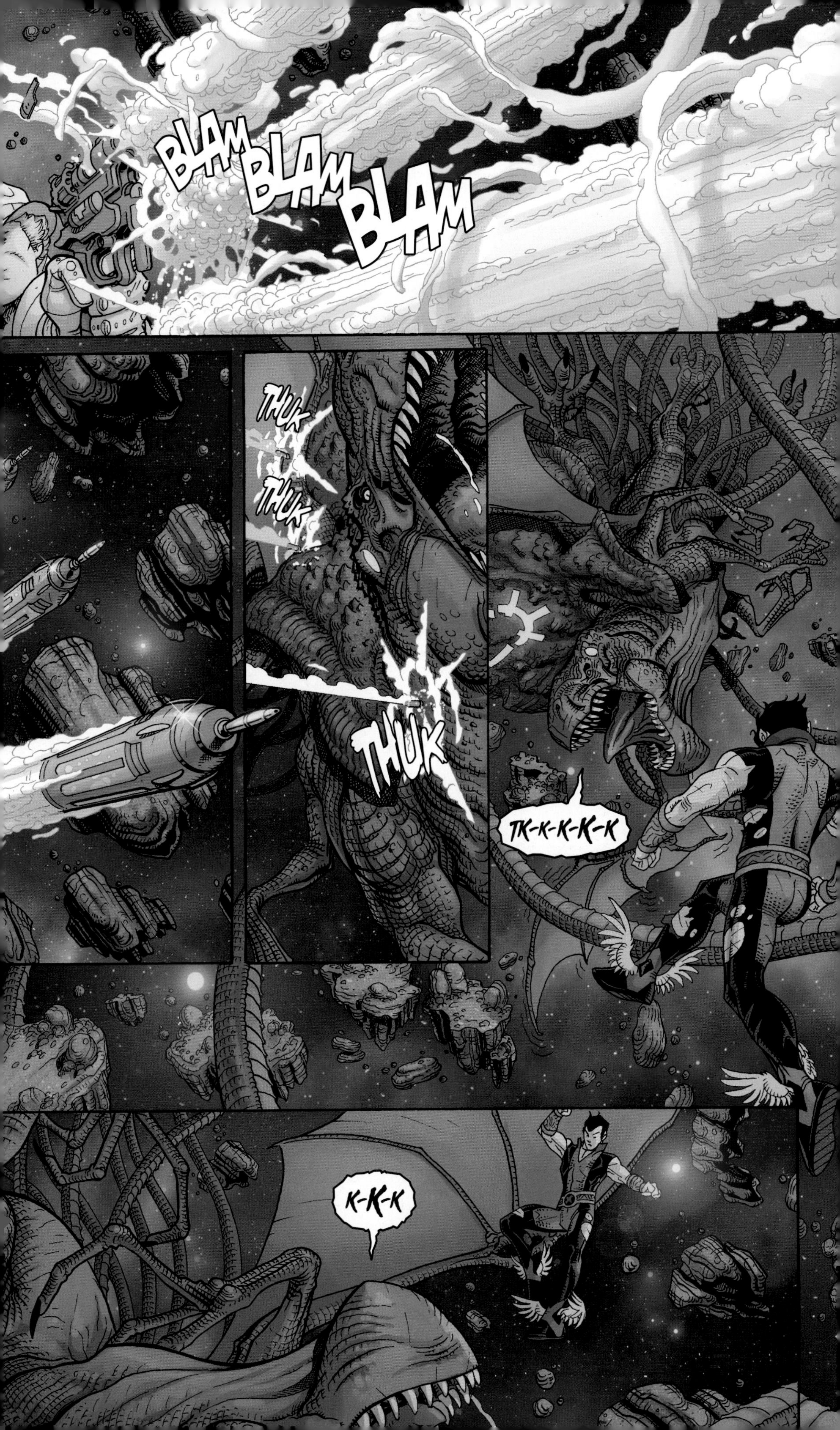
BLAM BLAM BLAM
THUK
THUK
THUK
TK-K-K-K-K
K-K-K

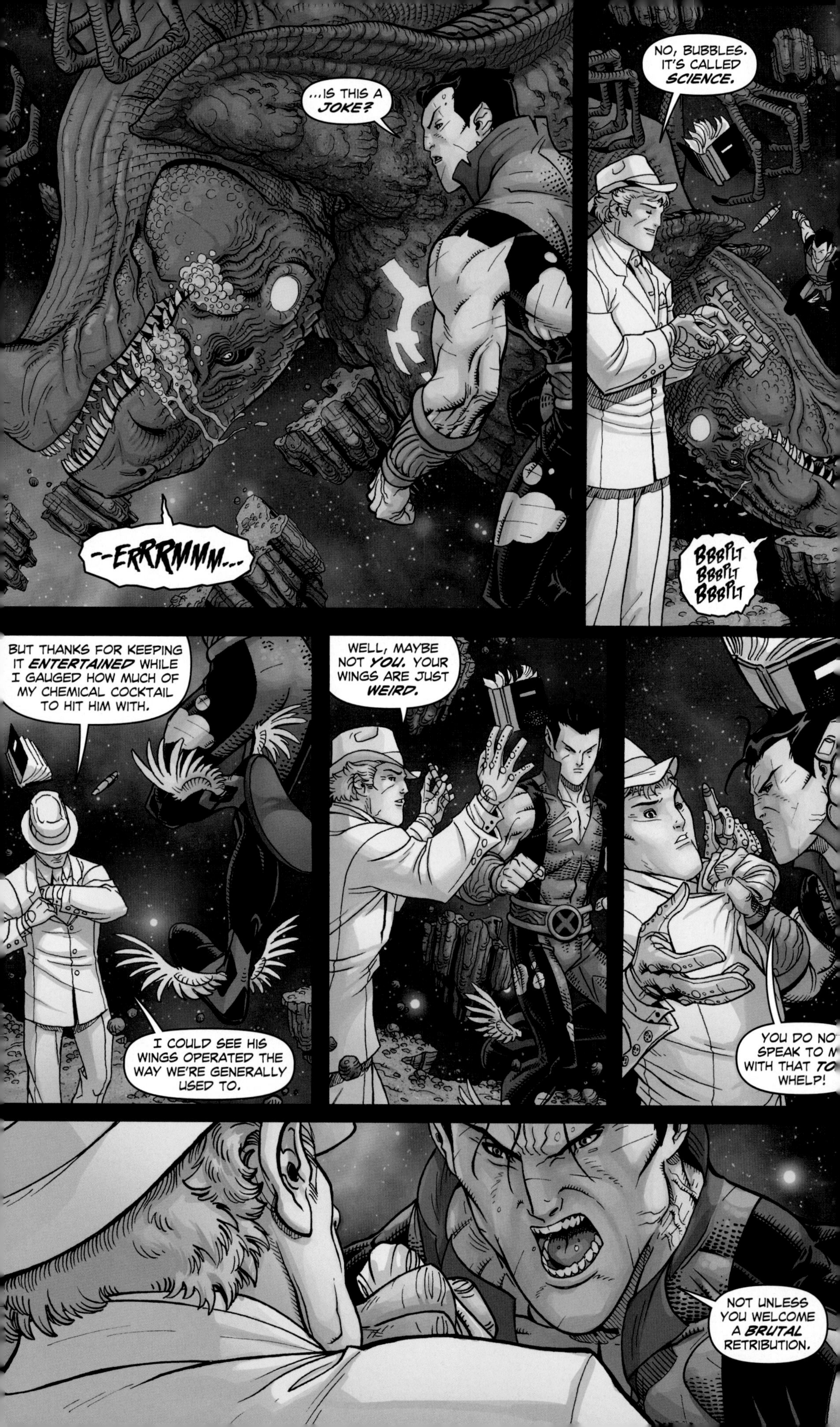
...IS THIS A JOKE?
--ERRRMMM...
NO, BUBBLES. IT'S CALLED SCIENCE.
BBBPLT BBBPLT BBBPLT
BUT THANKS FOR KEEPING IT ENTERTAINED WHILE I GAUGED HOW MUCH OF MY CHEMICAL COCKTAIL TO HIT HIM WITH.
I COULD SEE HIS WINGS OPERATED THE WAY WE'RE GENERALLY USED TO.
WELL, MAYBE NOT YOU. YOUR WINGS ARE JUST WEIRD.
YOU DO NO SPEAK TO M WITH THAT TO WHELP!
NOT UNLESS YOU WELCOME A BRUTAL RETRIBUTION.

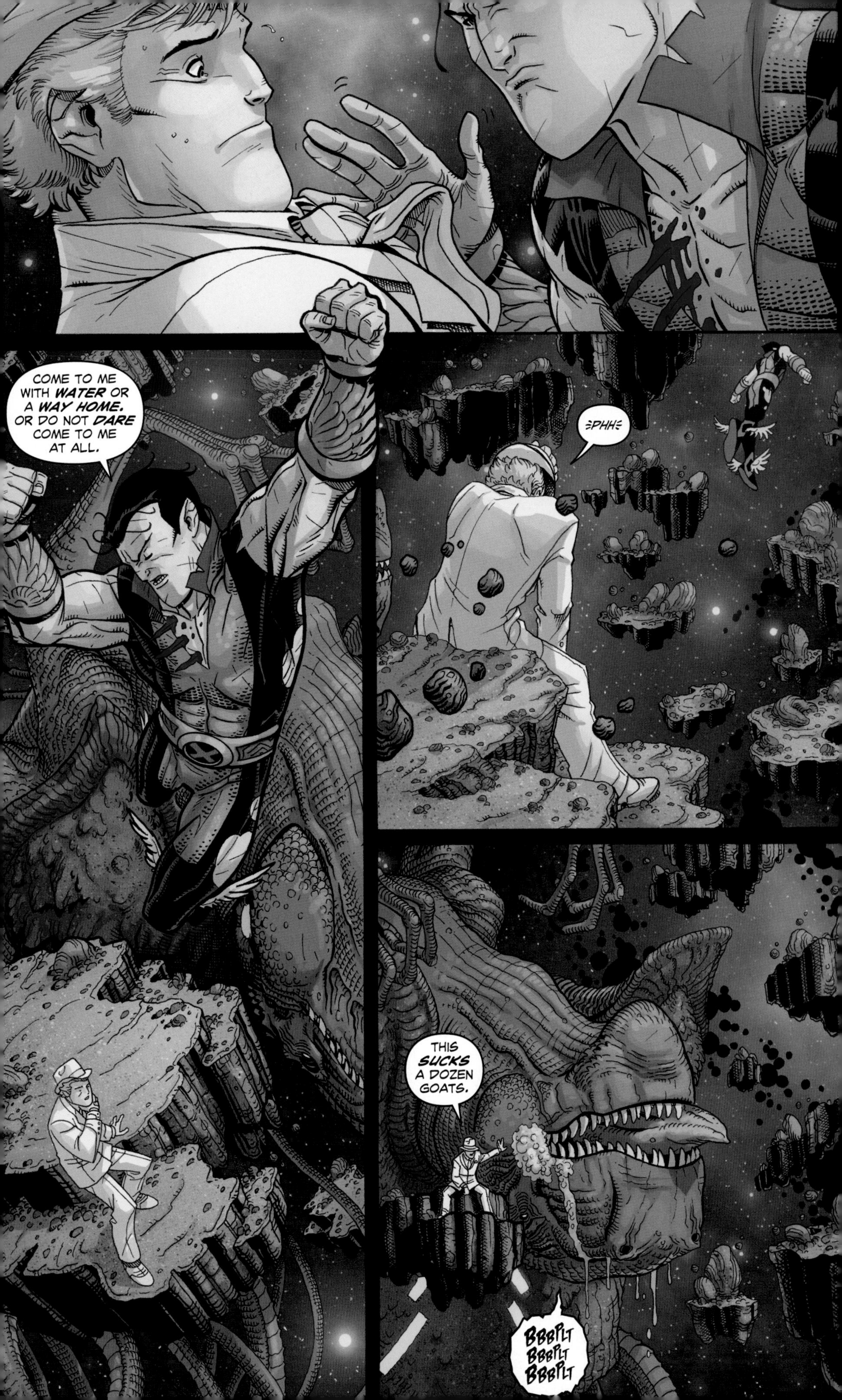
COME TO ME WITH WATER OR A WAY HOME. OR DO NOT DARE COME TO ME AT ALL.
PHH
THIS SUCKS A DOZEN GOATS.
BBBPLT BBBPLT BBBPLT

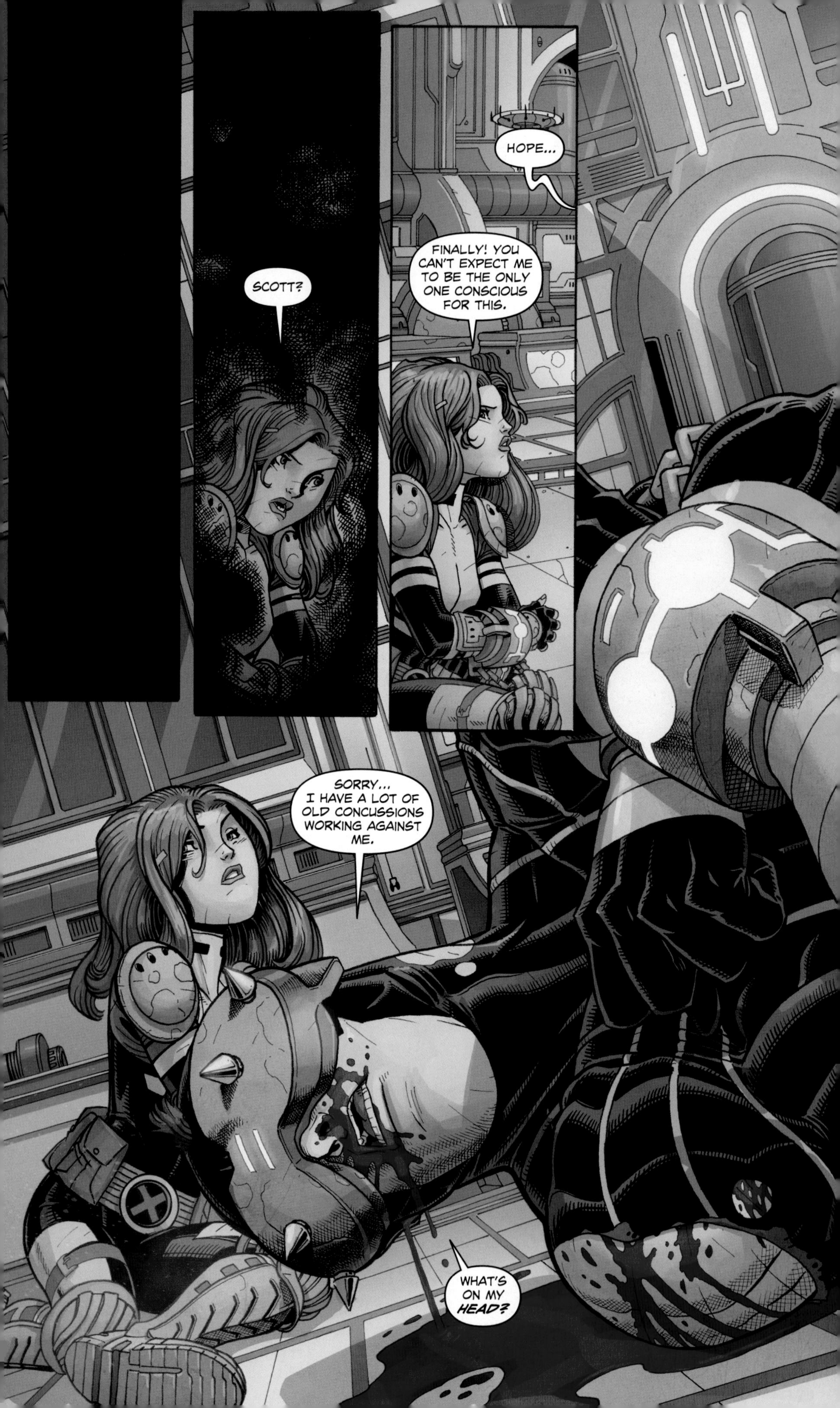
SCOTT?
HOPE...
FINALLY! YOU CAN'T EXPECT ME TO BE THE ONLY ONE CONSCIOUS FOR THIS.
SORRY... I HAVE A LOT OF OLD CONCUSSIONS WORKING AGAINST ME.
WHAT'S ON MY HEAD?

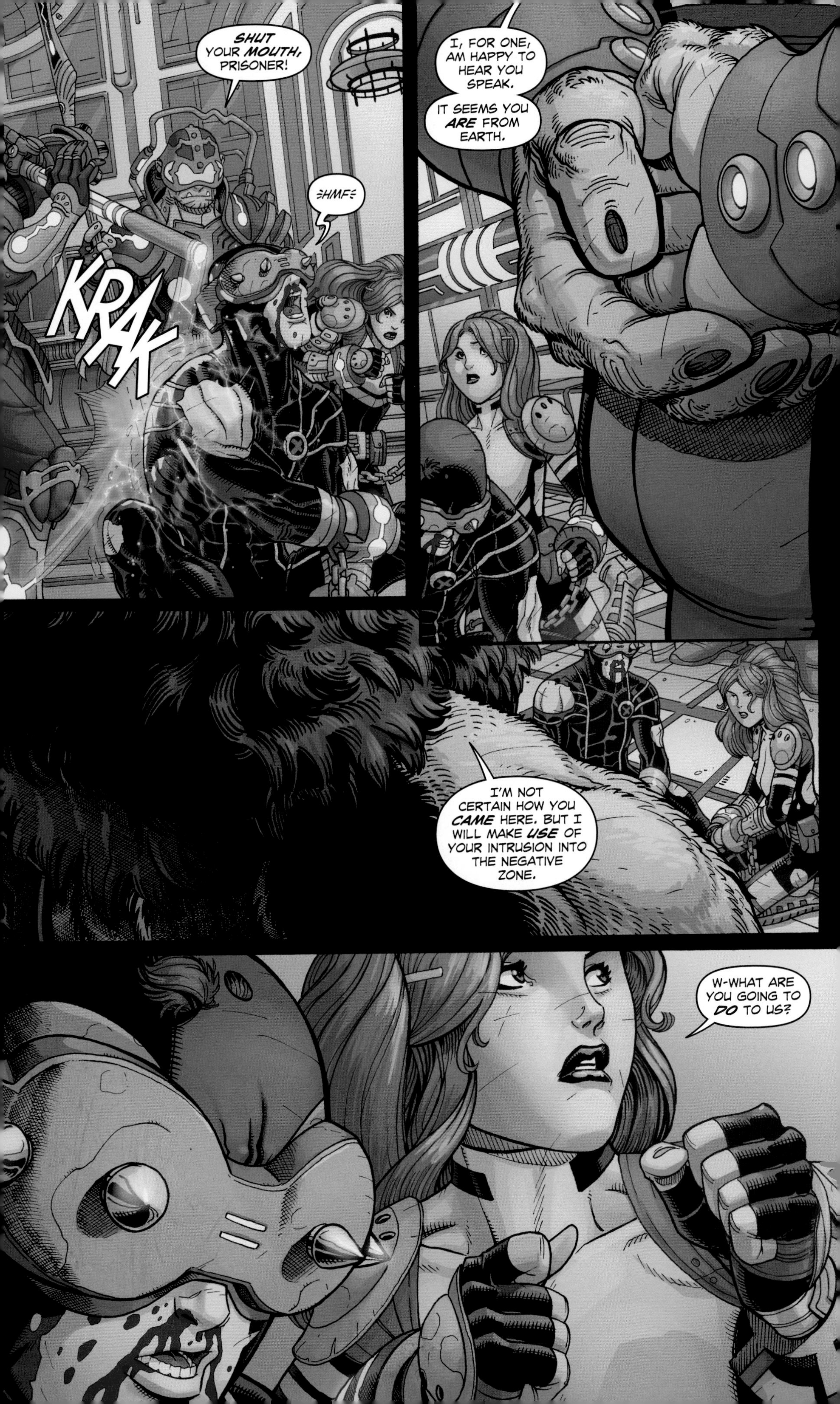
SHUT YOUR MOUTH, PRISONER!
HMF
KRAK
I, FOR ONE, AM HAPPY TO HEAR YOU SPEAK.
IT SEEMS YOU ARE FROM EARTH.
I'M NOT CERTAIN HOW YOU CAME HERE. BUT I WILL MAKE USE OF YOUR INTRUSION INTO THE NEGATIVE ZONE.
W-WHAT ARE YOU GOING TO DO TO US?

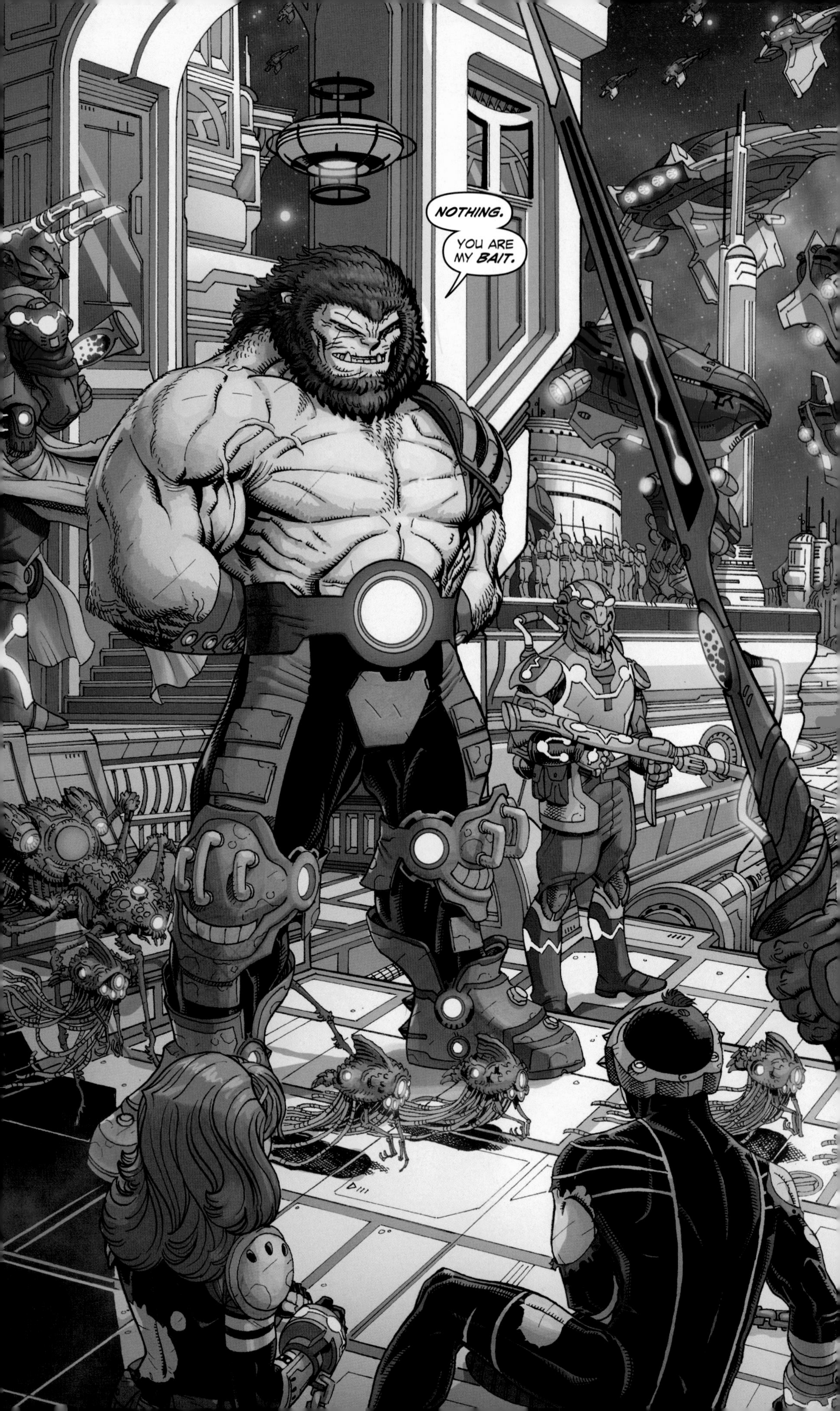
NOTHING.
YOU ARE MY BAIT.

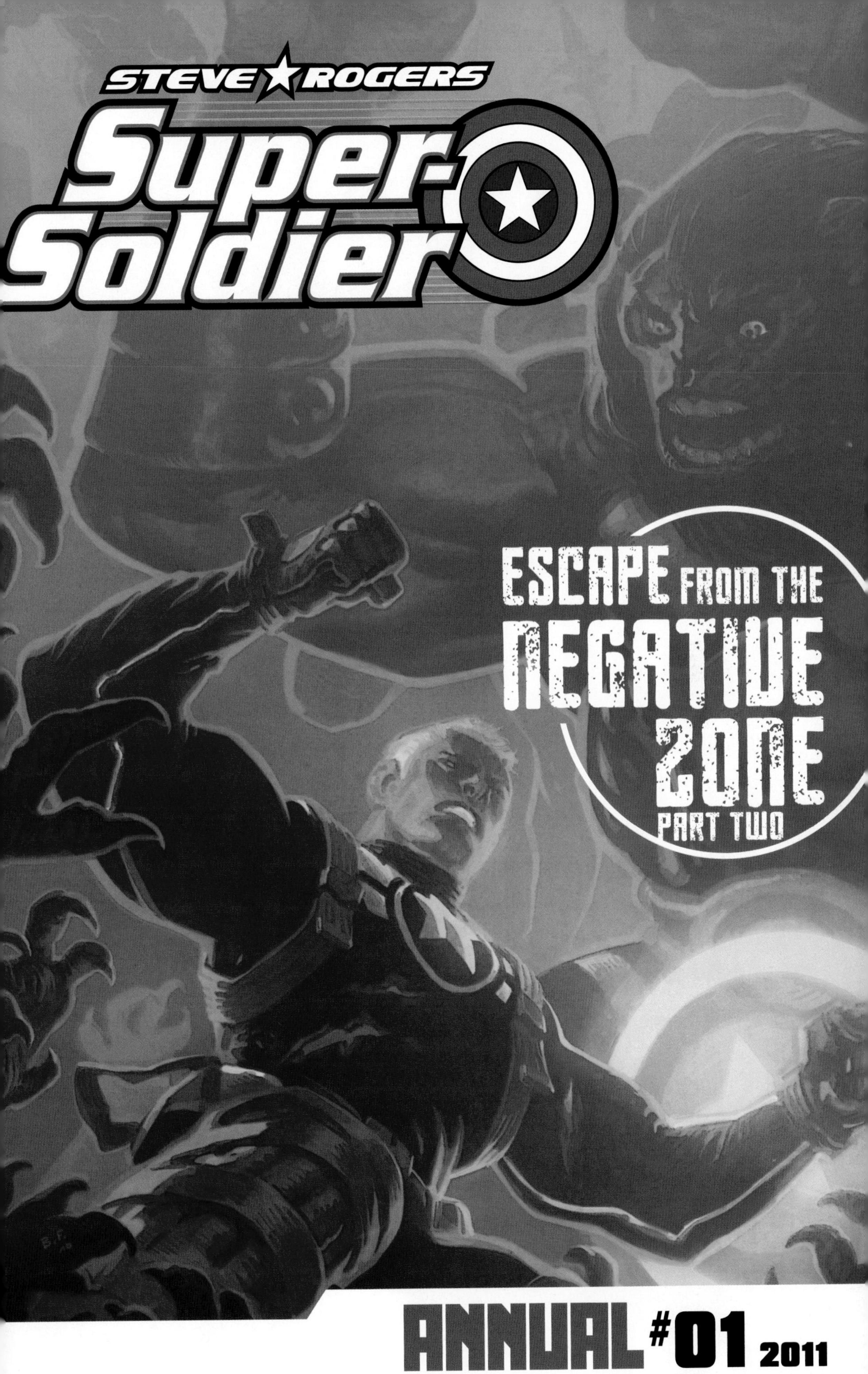
STEVE ROGERS
Super-Soldier
ESCAPE FROM THE NEGATIVE ZONE
PART TWO

ANNUAL #01 2011

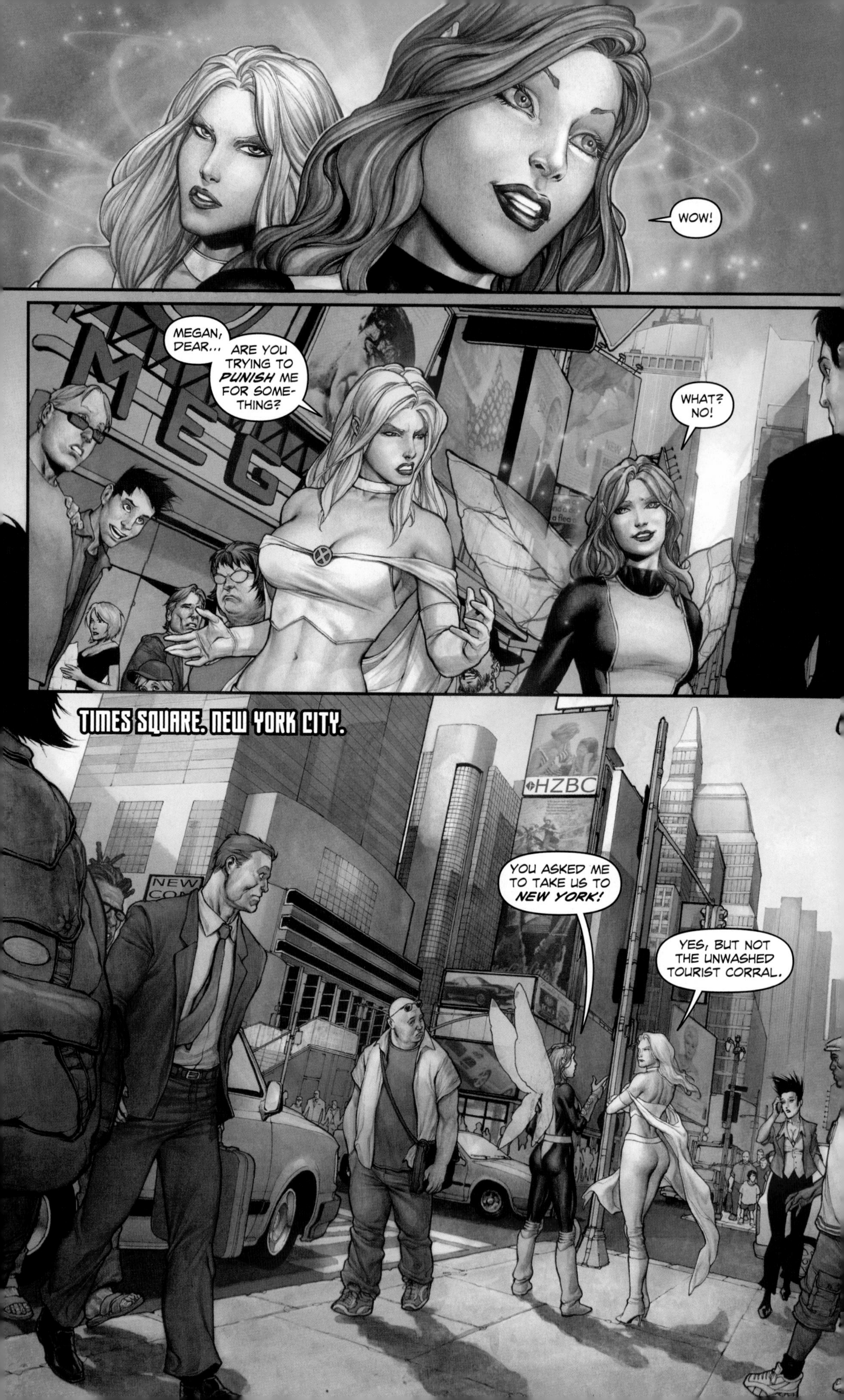
WOW!
MEGAN, DEAR...
ARE YOU TRYING TO *PUNISH* ME FOR SOME-THING?
WHAT? NO!
TIMES SQUARE. NEW YORK CITY.
YOU ASKED ME TO TAKE US TO *NEW YORK!*
YES, BUT NOT THE UNWASHED TOURIST CORRAL.
HZBC

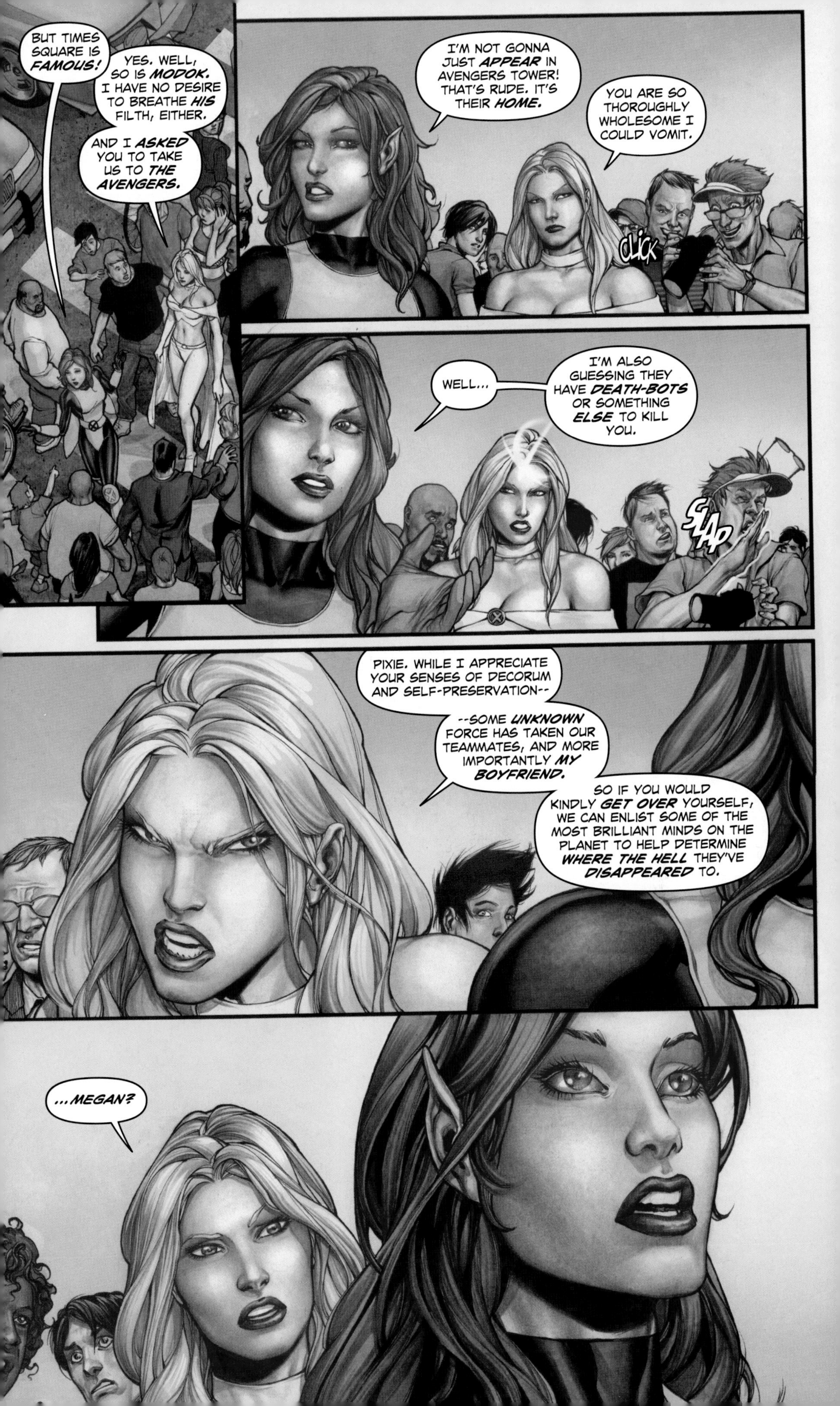

BUT TIMES SQUARE IS *FAMOUS!*
YES. WELL, SO IS *MODOK.* I HAVE NO DESIRE TO BREATHE *HIS* FILTH, EITHER.
AND I *ASKED* YOU TO TAKE US TO *THE AVENGERS.*
I'M NOT GONNA JUST *APPEAR* IN AVENGERS TOWER! THAT'S RUDE. IT'S THEIR *HOME.*
YOU ARE SO THOROUGHLY WHOLESOME I COULD VOMIT.
CLICK
WELL...
I'M ALSO GUESSING THEY HAVE *DEATH-BOTS* OR SOMETHING *ELSE* TO KILL YOU.
SLAP
PIXIE. WHILE I APPRECIATE YOUR SENSES OF DECORUM AND SELF-PRESERVATION--
--SOME *UNKNOWN* FORCE HAS TAKEN OUR TEAMMATES, AND MORE IMPORTANTLY *MY BOYFRIEND.*
SO IF YOU WOULD KINDLY *GET OVER* YOURSELF, WE CAN ENLIST SOME OF THE MOST BRILLIANT MINDS ON THE PLANET TO HELP DETERMINE *WHERE THE HELL* THEY'VE *DISAPPEARED* TO.
...MEGAN?

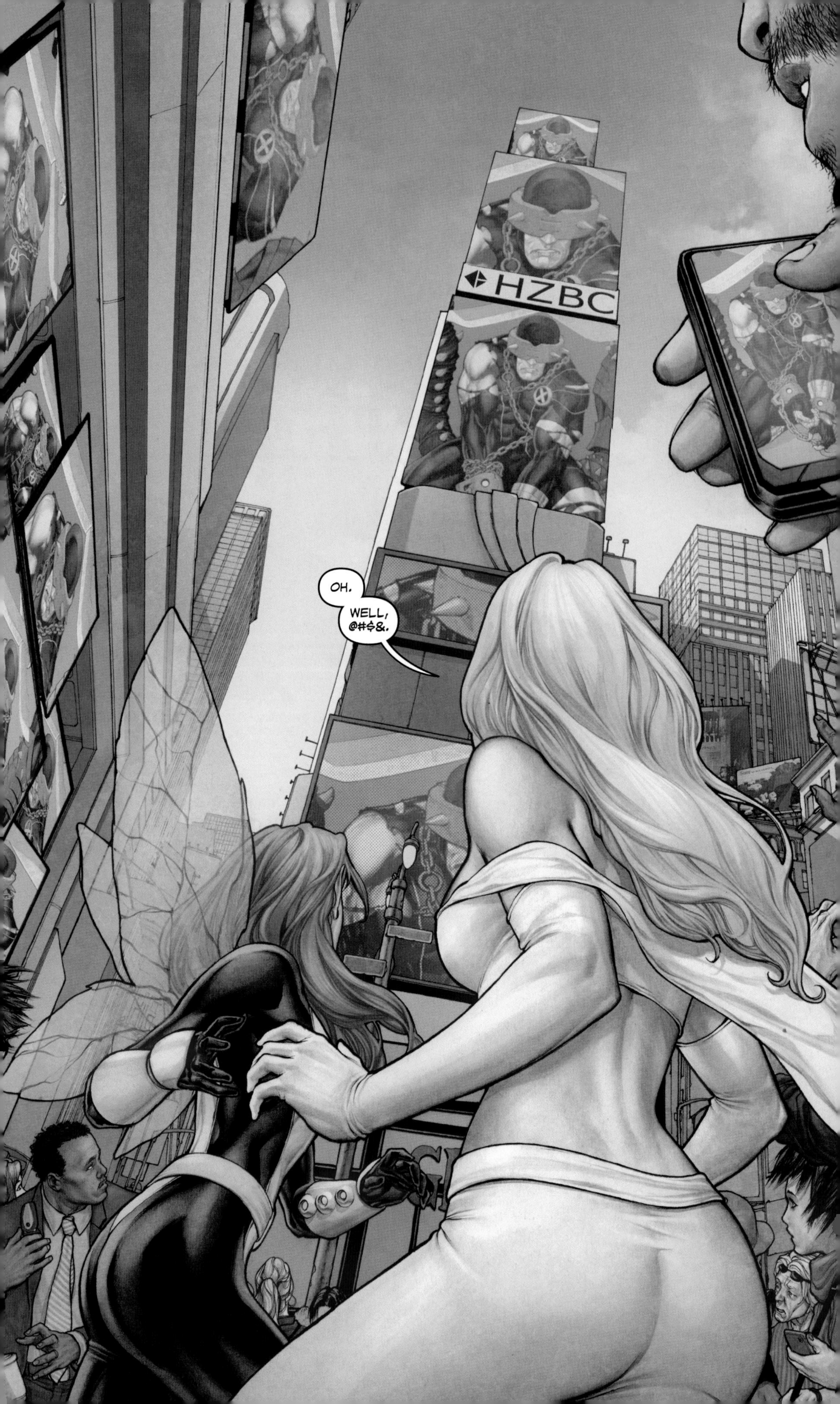
HZBC
OH.
WELL, @#$&.

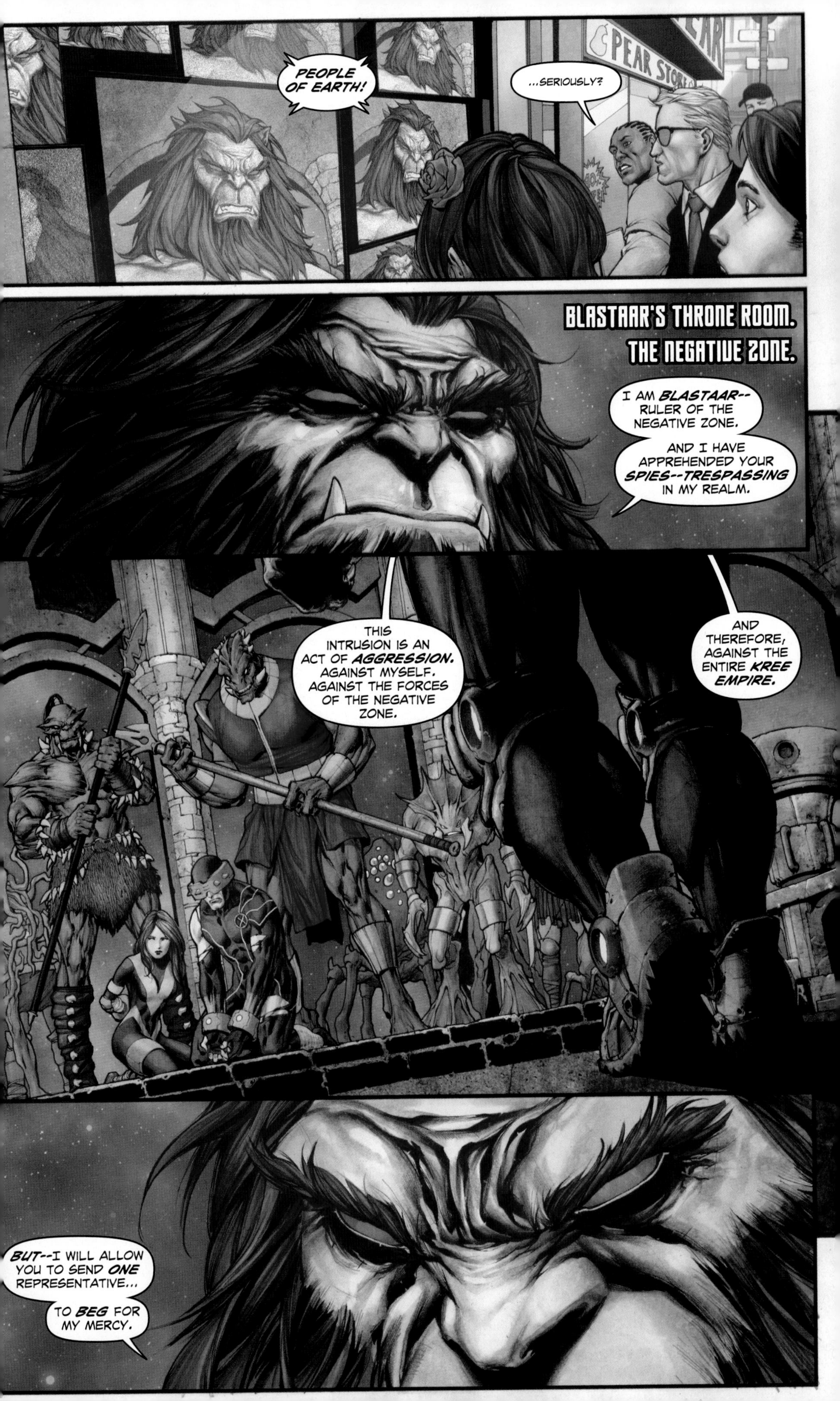
PEOPLE OF EARTH!
...SERIOUSLY?
PEAR STORE
BLASTAAR'S THRONE ROOM.
THE NEGATIVE ZONE.
I AM BLASTAAR-- RULER OF THE NEGATIVE ZONE.
AND I HAVE APPREHENDED YOUR SPIES--TRESPASSING IN MY REALM.
THIS INTRUSION IS AN ACT OF AGGRESSION. AGAINST MYSELF. AGAINST THE FORCES OF THE NEGATIVE ZONE.
AND THEREFORE, AGAINST THE ENTIRE KREE EMPIRE.
BUT--I WILL ALLOW YOU TO SEND ONE REPRESENTATIVE...
TO BEG FOR MY MERCY.

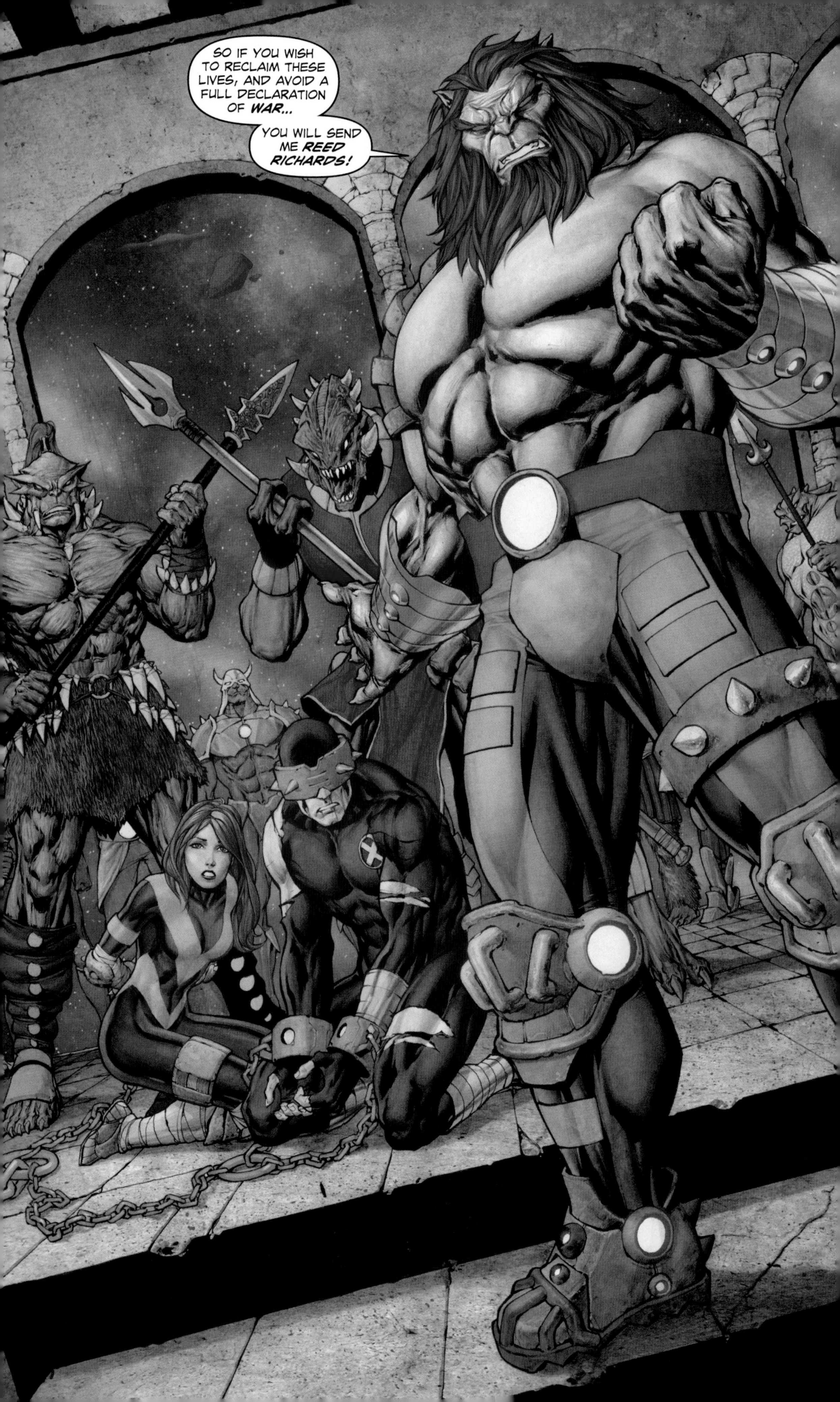
SO IF YOU WISH TO RECLAIM THESE LIVES, AND AVOID A FULL DECLARATION OF WAR...
YOU WILL SEND ME REED RICHARDS!

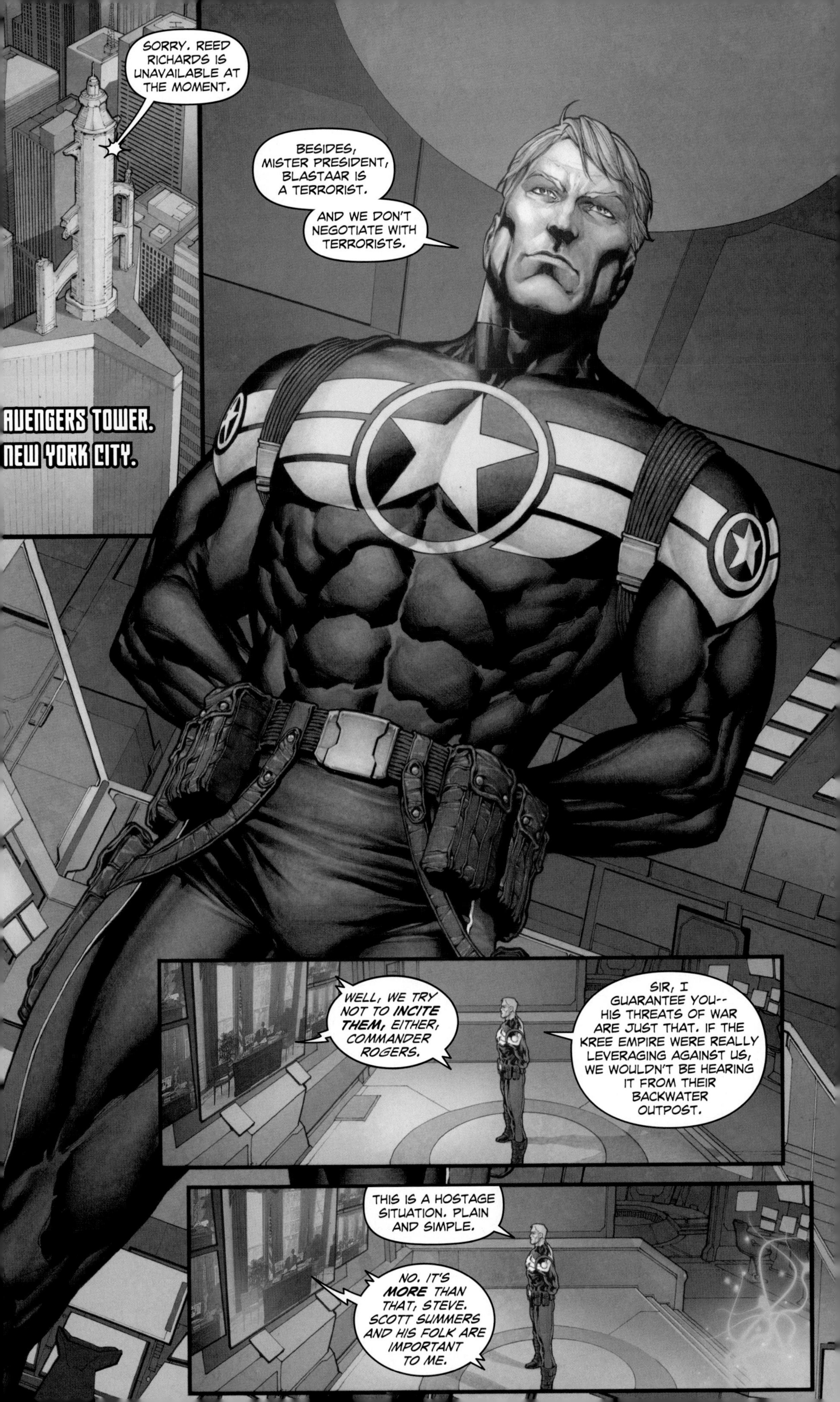
SORRY. REED RICHARDS IS UNAVAILABLE AT THE MOMENT.
AVENGERS TOWER. NEW YORK CITY.
BESIDES, MISTER PRESIDENT, BLASTAAR IS A TERRORIST.
AND WE DON'T NEGOTIATE WITH TERRORISTS.
WELL, WE TRY NOT TO INCITE THEM, EITHER, COMMANDER ROGERS.
SIR, I GUARANTEE YOU-- HIS THREATS OF WAR ARE JUST THAT. IF THE KREE EMPIRE WERE REALLY LEVERAGING AGAINST US, WE WOULDN'T BE HEARING IT FROM THEIR BACKWATER OUTPOST.
THIS IS A HOSTAGE SITUATION. PLAIN AND SIMPLE.
NO. IT'S MORE THAN THAT, STEVE. SCOTT SUMMERS AND HIS FOLK ARE IMPORTANT TO ME.

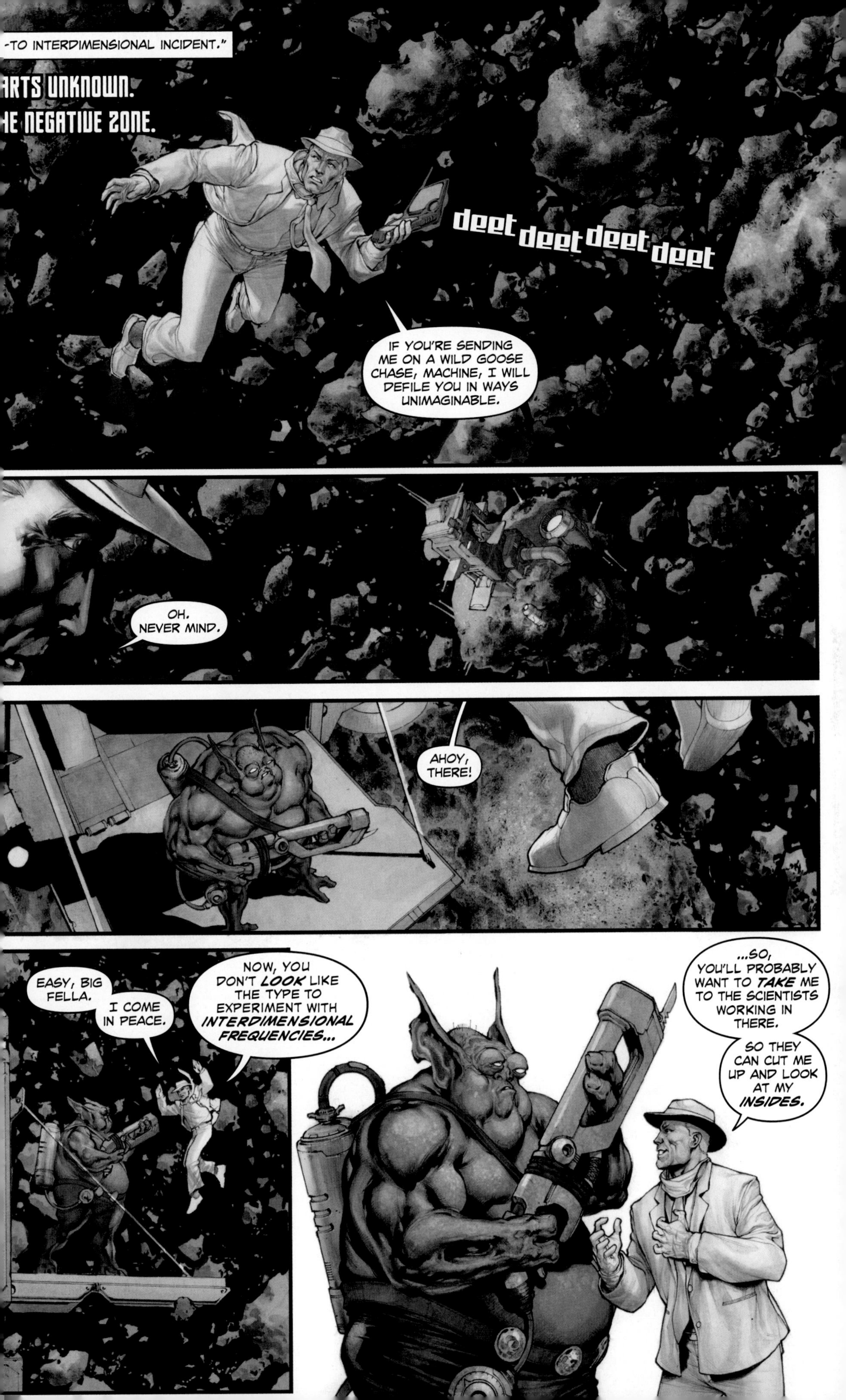
-TO INTERDIMENSIONAL INCIDENT."
ARTS UNKNOWN.
HE NEGATIVE ZONE.
deet deet deet deet
IF YOU'RE SENDING ME ON A WILD GOOSE CHASE, MACHINE, I WILL DEFILE YOU IN WAYS UNIMAGINABLE.
OH. NEVER MIND.
AHOY, THERE!
EASY, BIG FELLA.
I COME IN PEACE.
NOW, YOU DON'T LOOK LIKE THE TYPE TO EXPERIMENT WITH INTERDIMENSIONAL FREQUENCIES...
...SO, YOU'LL PROBABLY WANT TO TAKE ME TO THE SCIENTISTS WORKING IN THERE.
SO THEY CAN CUT ME UP AND LOOK AT MY INSIDES.

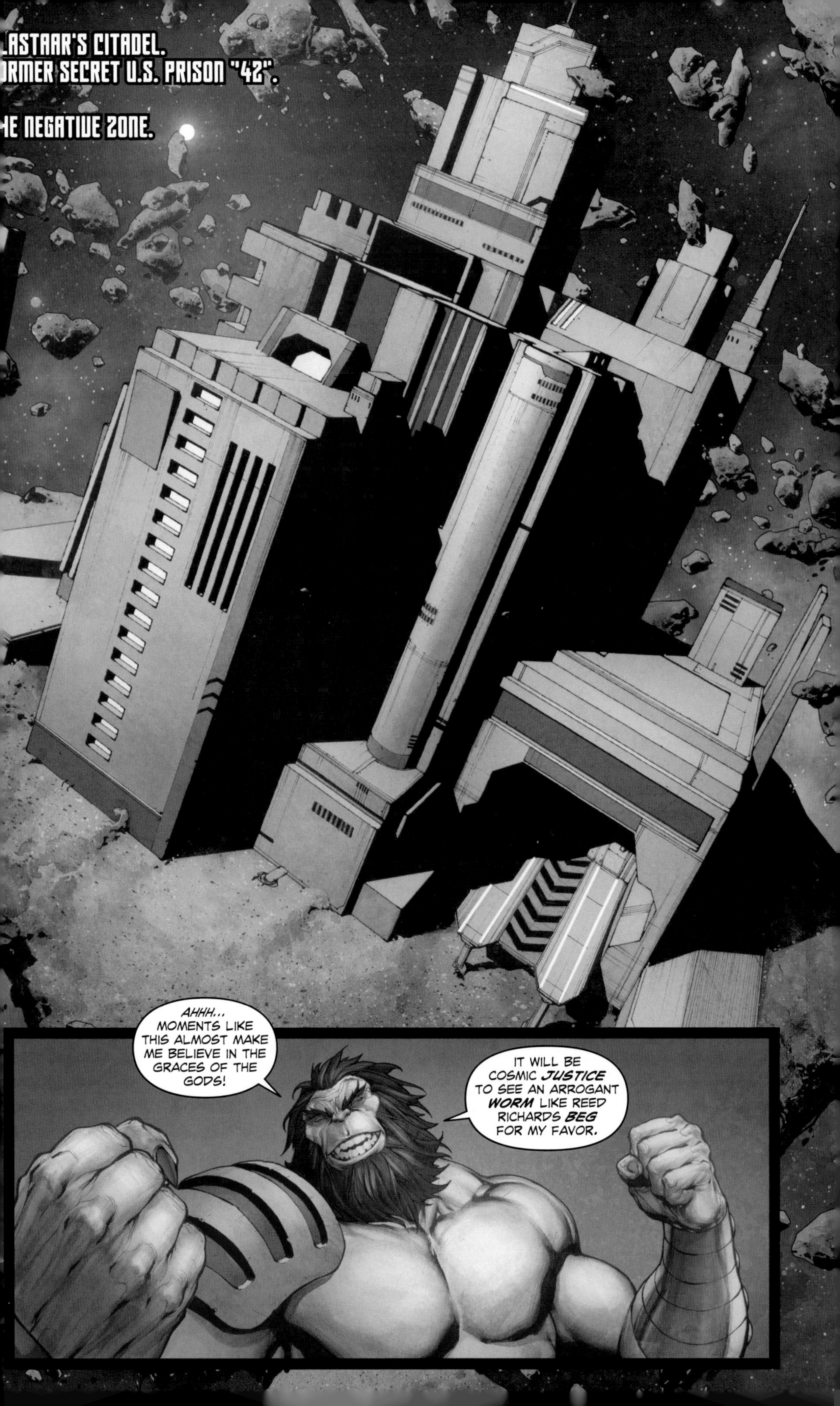

LASTAAR'S CITADEL.
ORMER SECRET U.S. PRISON "42".
HE NEGATIVE ZONE.
AHHH... MOMENTS LIKE THIS ALMOST MAKE ME BELIEVE IN THE GRACES OF THE GODS!
IT WILL BE COSMIC JUSTICE TO SEE AN ARROGANT WORM LIKE REED RICHARDS BEG FOR MY FAVOR.

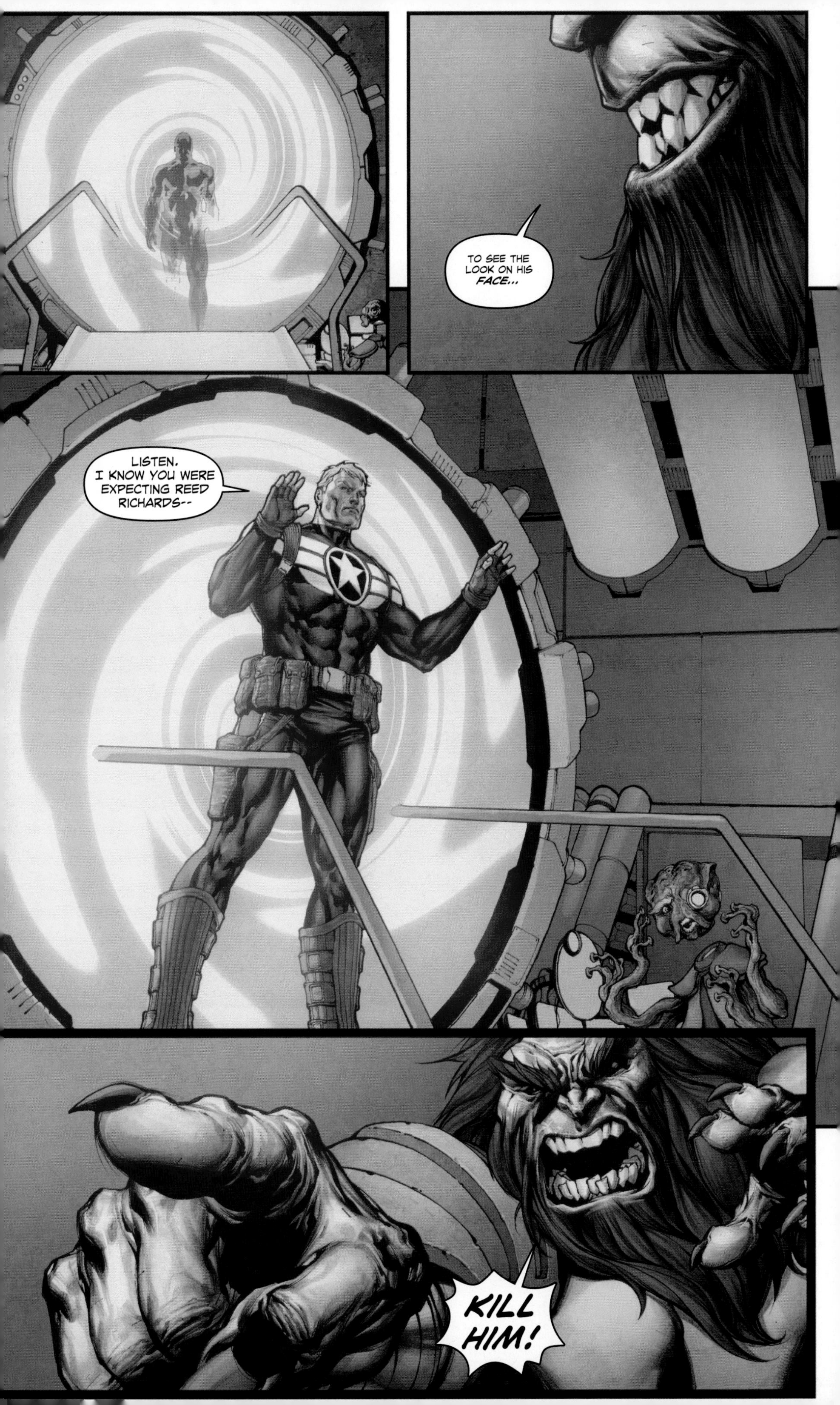
TO SEE THE LOOK ON HIS *FACE...*
LISTEN. I KNOW YOU WERE EXPECTING REED RICHARDS--
KILL HIM!

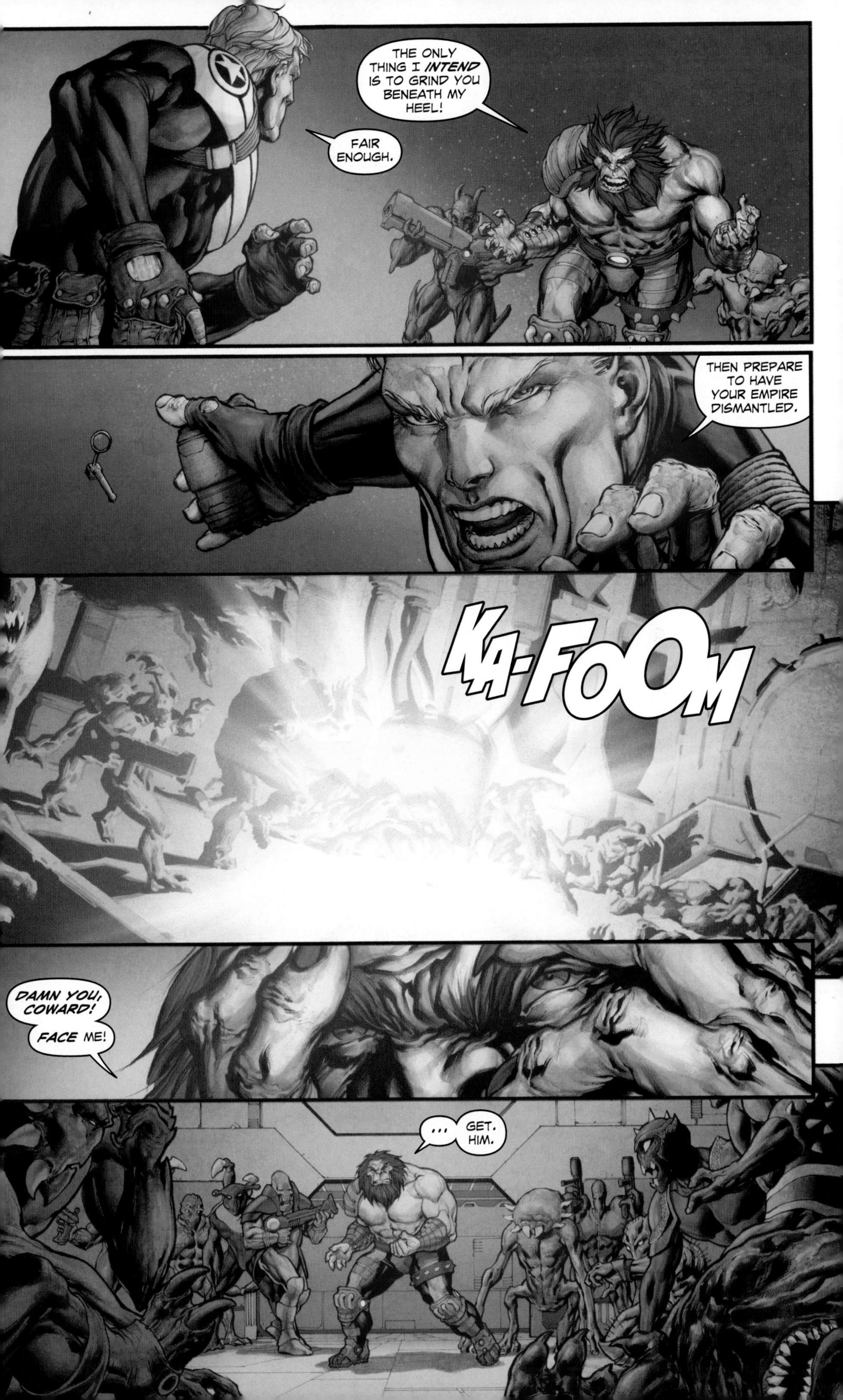
THE ONLY THING I *INTEND* IS TO GRIND YOU BENEATH MY HEEL!
FAIR ENOUGH.
THEN PREPARE TO HAVE YOUR EMPIRE DISMANTLED.
KA-FOOM
DAMN YOU, COWARD!
FACE ME!
...
GET. HIM.

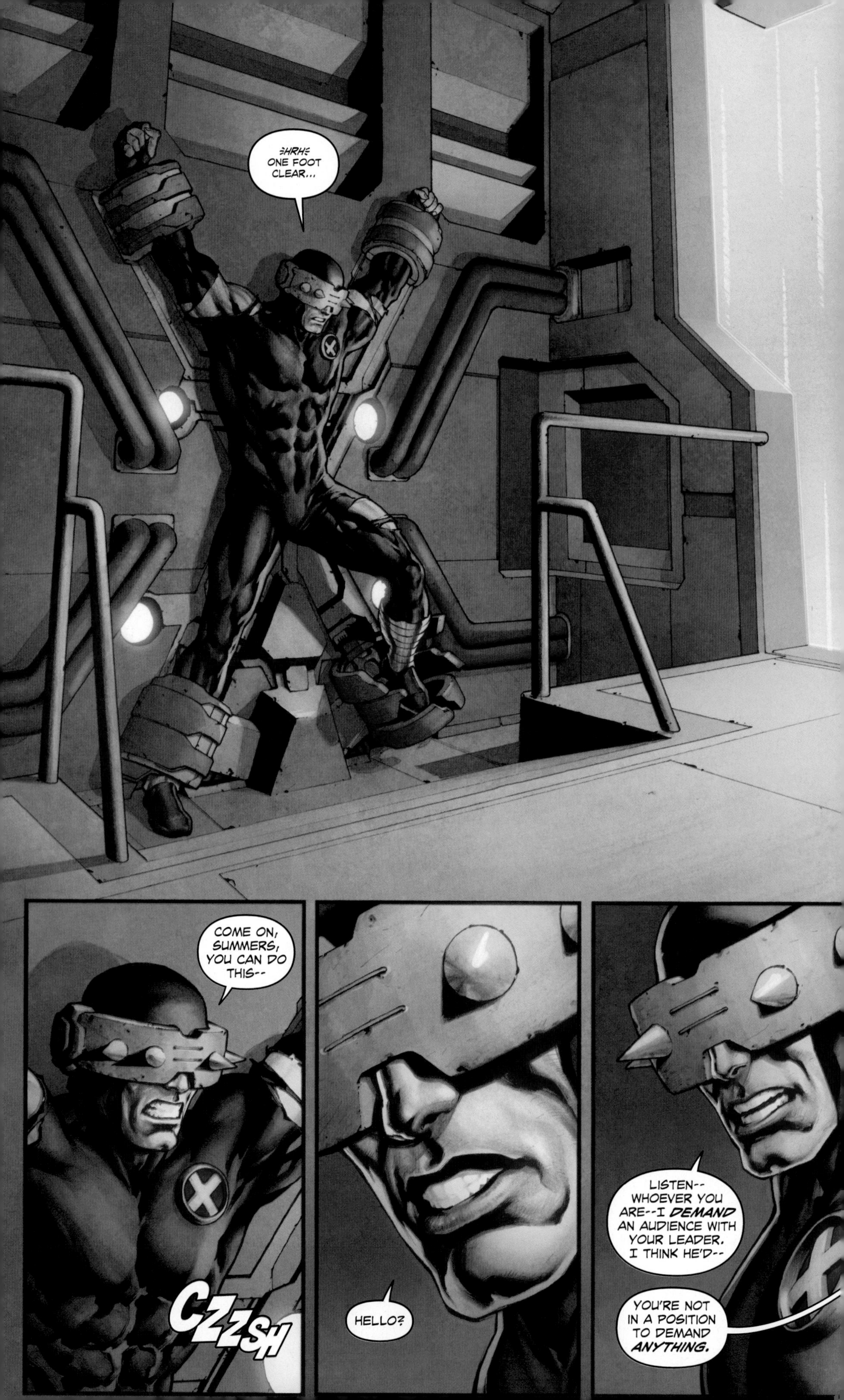

=HRH= ONE FOOT CLEAR...
COME ON, SUMMERS, YOU CAN DO THIS--
CZZSH
HELLO?
LISTEN-- WHOEVER YOU ARE--I DEMAND AN AUDIENCE WITH YOUR LEADER. I THINK HE'D--
YOU'RE NOT IN A POSITION TO DEMAND ANYTHING.

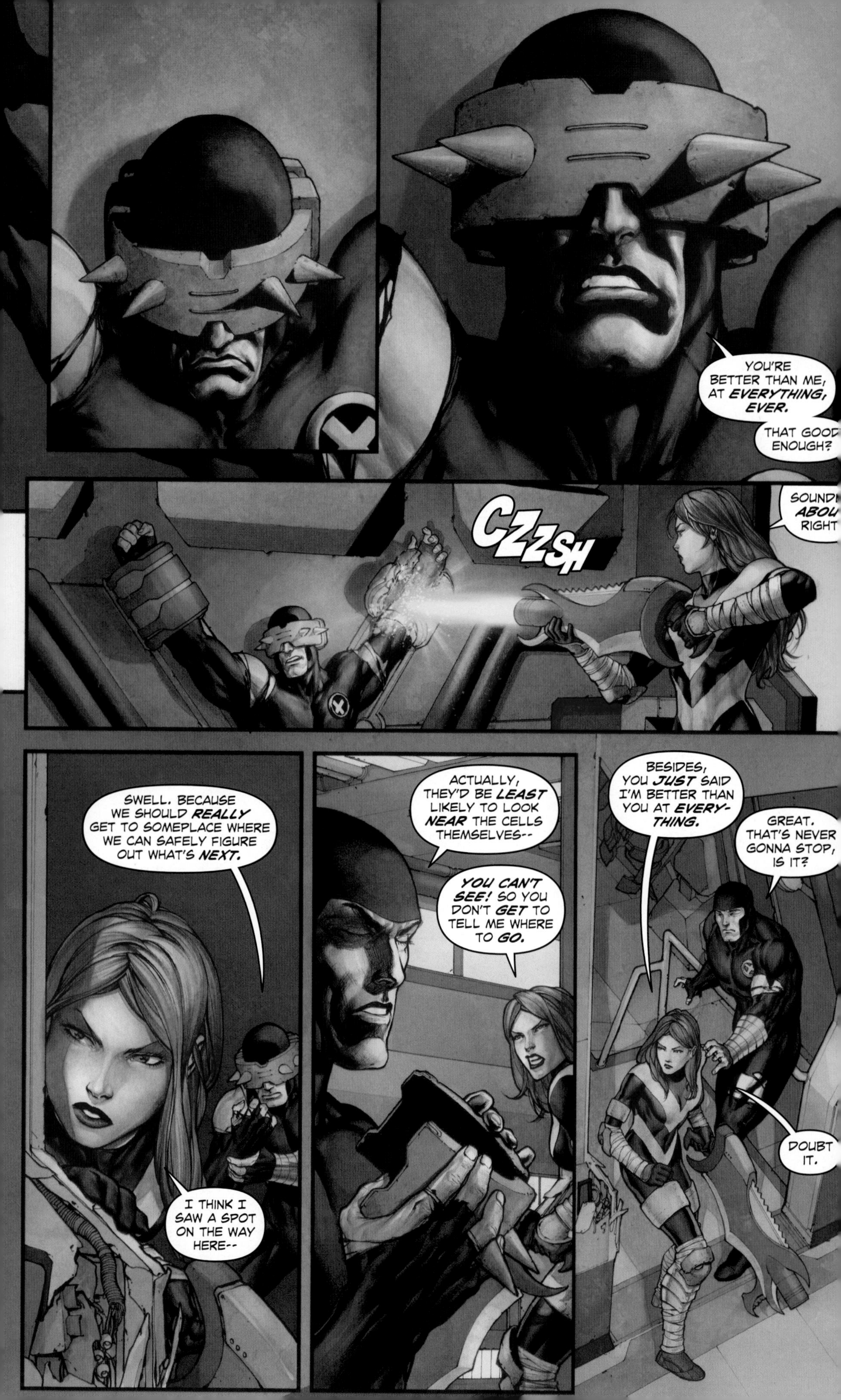

YOU'RE BETTER THAN ME, AT EVERYTHING, EVER.
THAT GOOD ENOUGH?
SOUND ABOU RIGHT
CZZSH
SWELL. BECAUSE WE SHOULD REALLY GET TO SOMEPLACE WHERE WE CAN SAFELY FIGURE OUT WHAT'S NEXT.
I THINK I SAW A SPOT ON THE WAY HERE--
ACTUALLY, THEY'D BE LEAST LIKELY TO LOOK NEAR THE CELLS THEMSELVES--
YOU CAN'T SEE! SO YOU DON'T GET TO TELL ME WHERE TO GO.
BESIDES, YOU JUST SAID I'M BETTER THAN YOU AT EVERY-THING.
GREAT. THAT'S NEVER GONNA STOP, IS IT?
DOUBT IT.

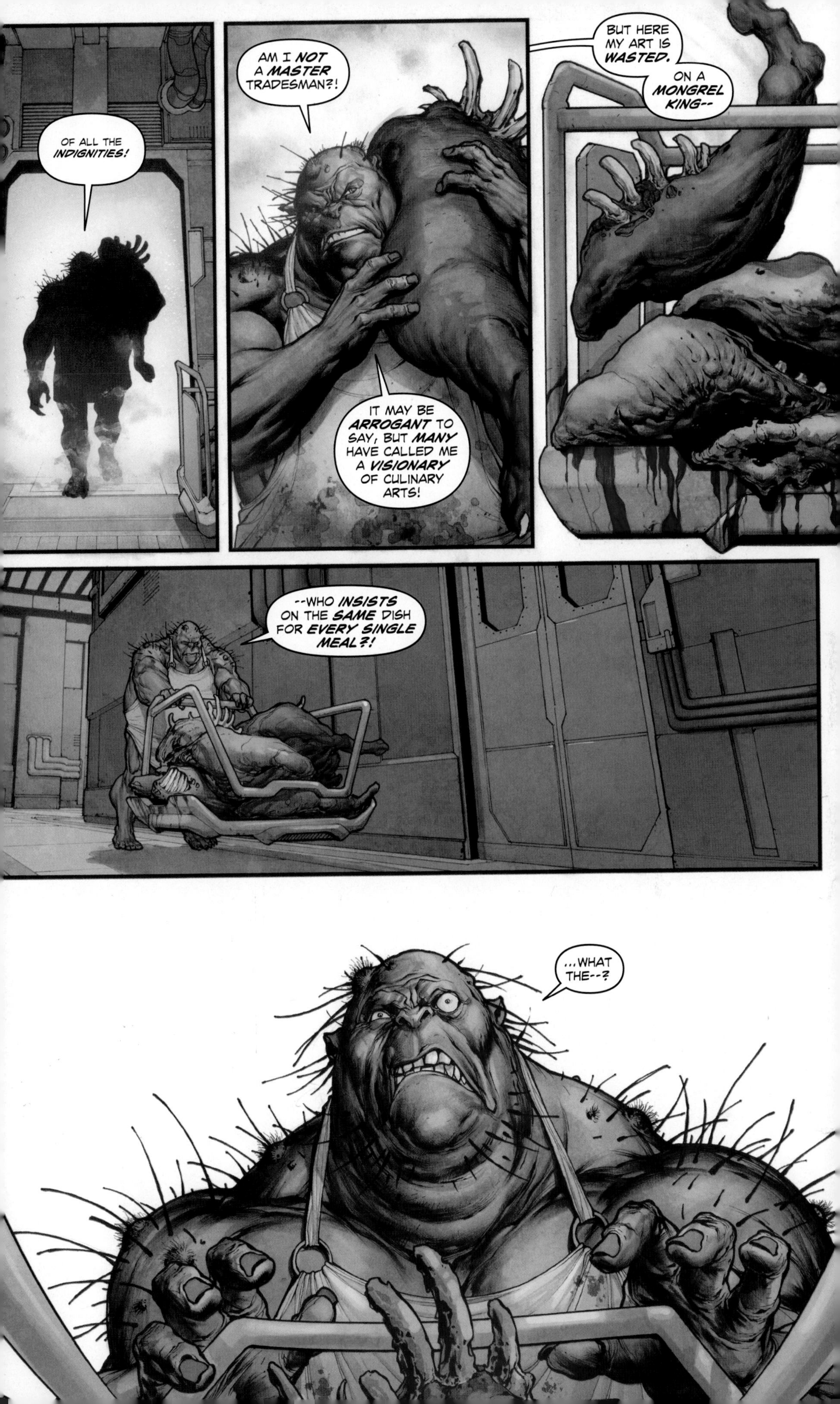

OF ALL THE INDIGNITIES!
AM I NOT A MASTER TRADESMAN?!
IT MAY BE ARROGANT TO SAY, BUT MANY HAVE CALLED ME A VISIONARY OF CULINARY ARTS!
BUT HERE MY ART IS WASTED.
ON A MONGREL KING--
--WHO INSISTS ON THE SAME DISH FOR EVERY SINGLE MEAL?!
...WHAT THE--?

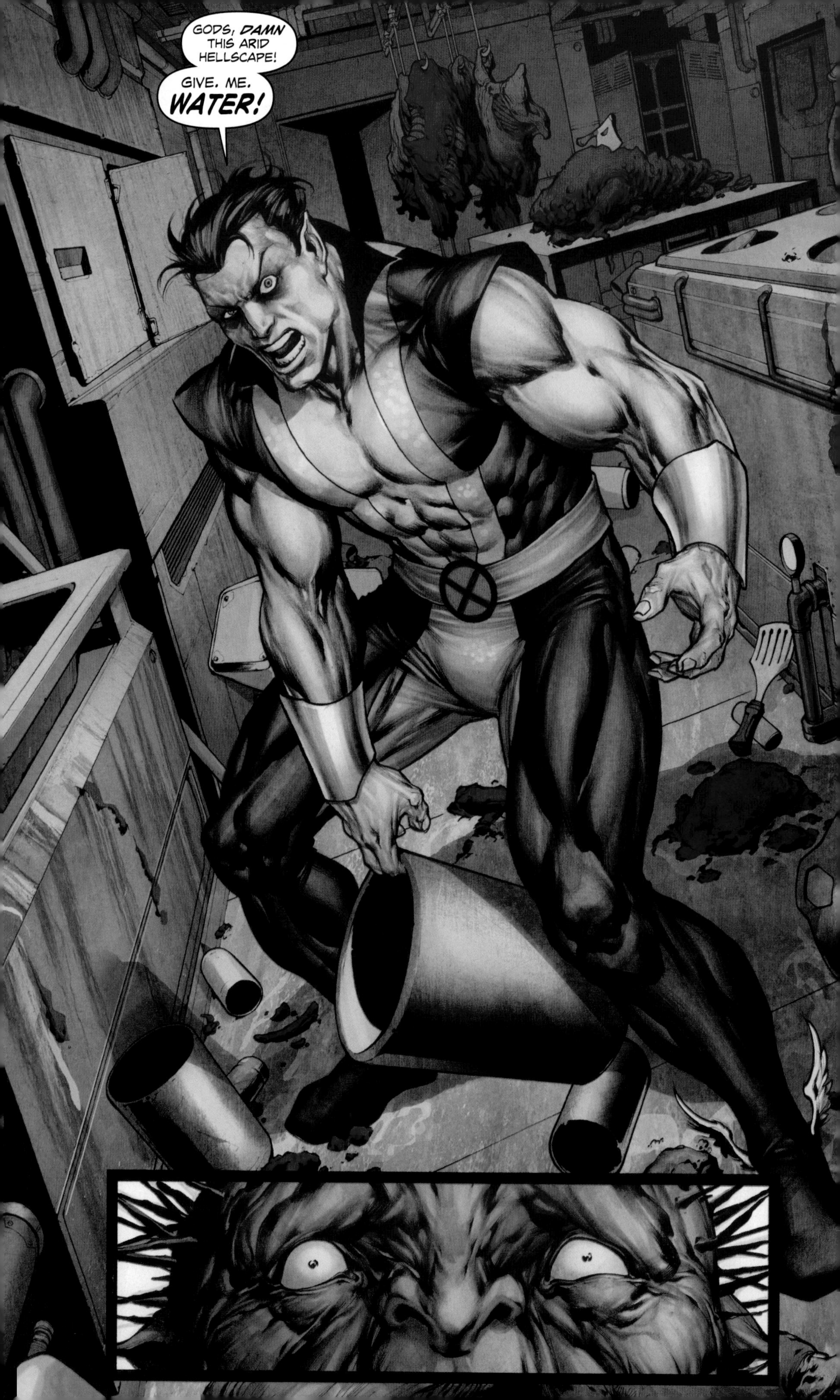
GODS, DAMN THIS ARID HELLSCAPE!
GIVE. ME. WATER!

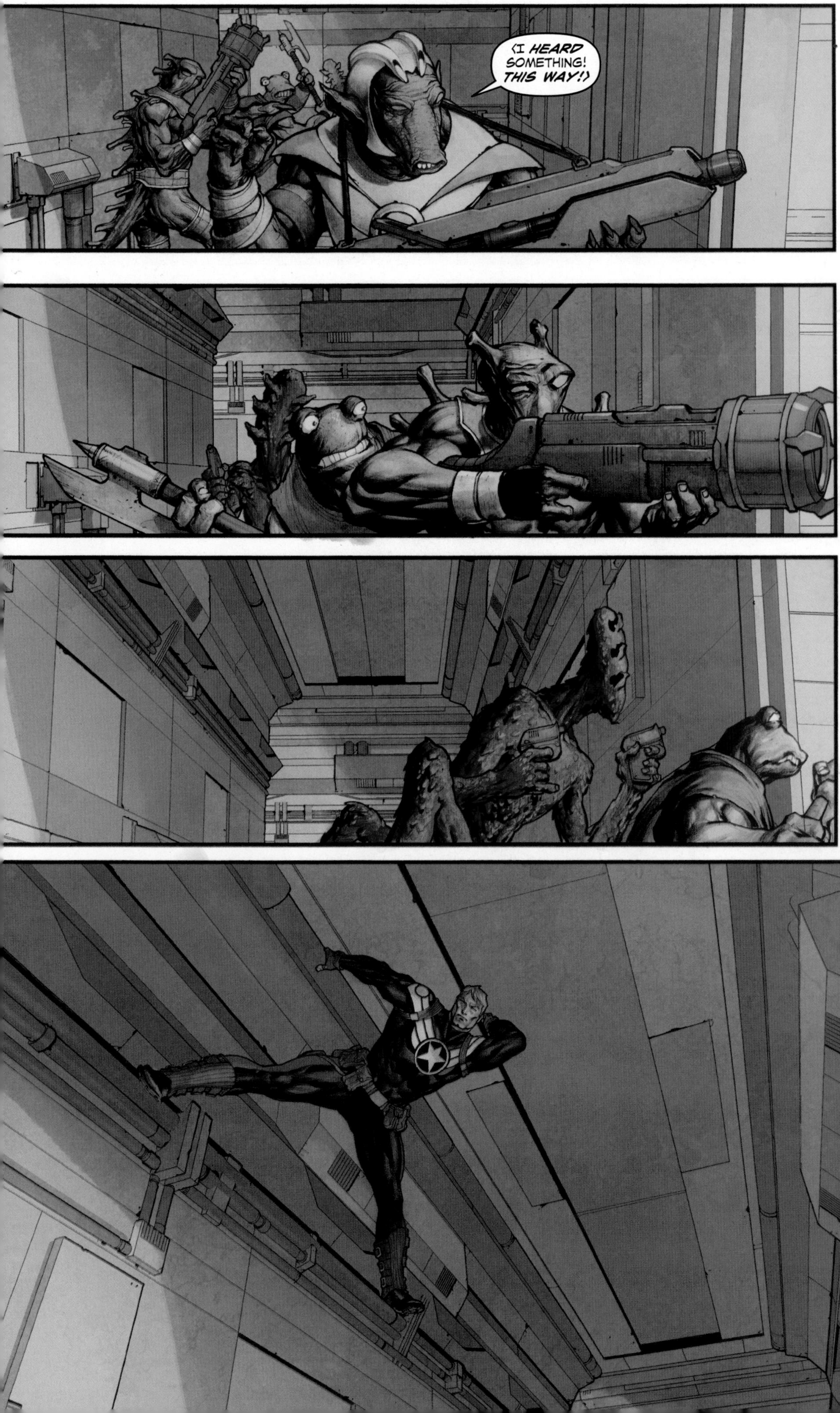
‹I *HEARD* SOMETHING! *THIS WAY!*›

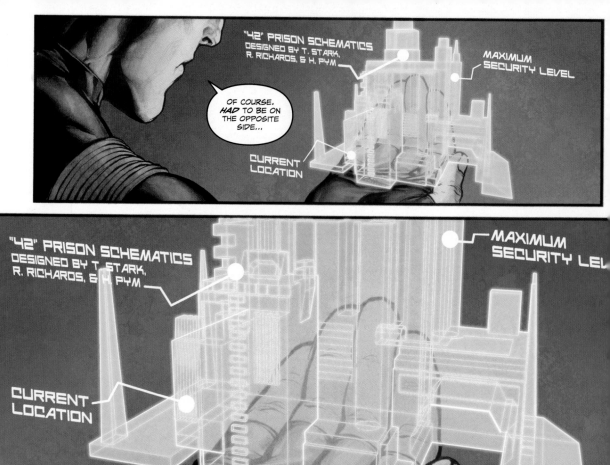

"42" PRISON SCHEMATICS
DESIGNED BY T. STARK,
R. RICHARDS, & H. PYM

MAXIMUM
SECURITY LEVEL

OF COURSE, *HAD* TO BE ON THE OPPOSITE SIDE...

CURRENT LOCATION

"42" PRISON SCHEMATICS
DESIGNED BY T. STARK,
R. RICHARDS, & H. PYM

MAXIMUM
SECURITY LEV

CURRENT
LOCATION

I CAN'T *WAIT* FOR THIS PLACE TO GET DESTROYED.

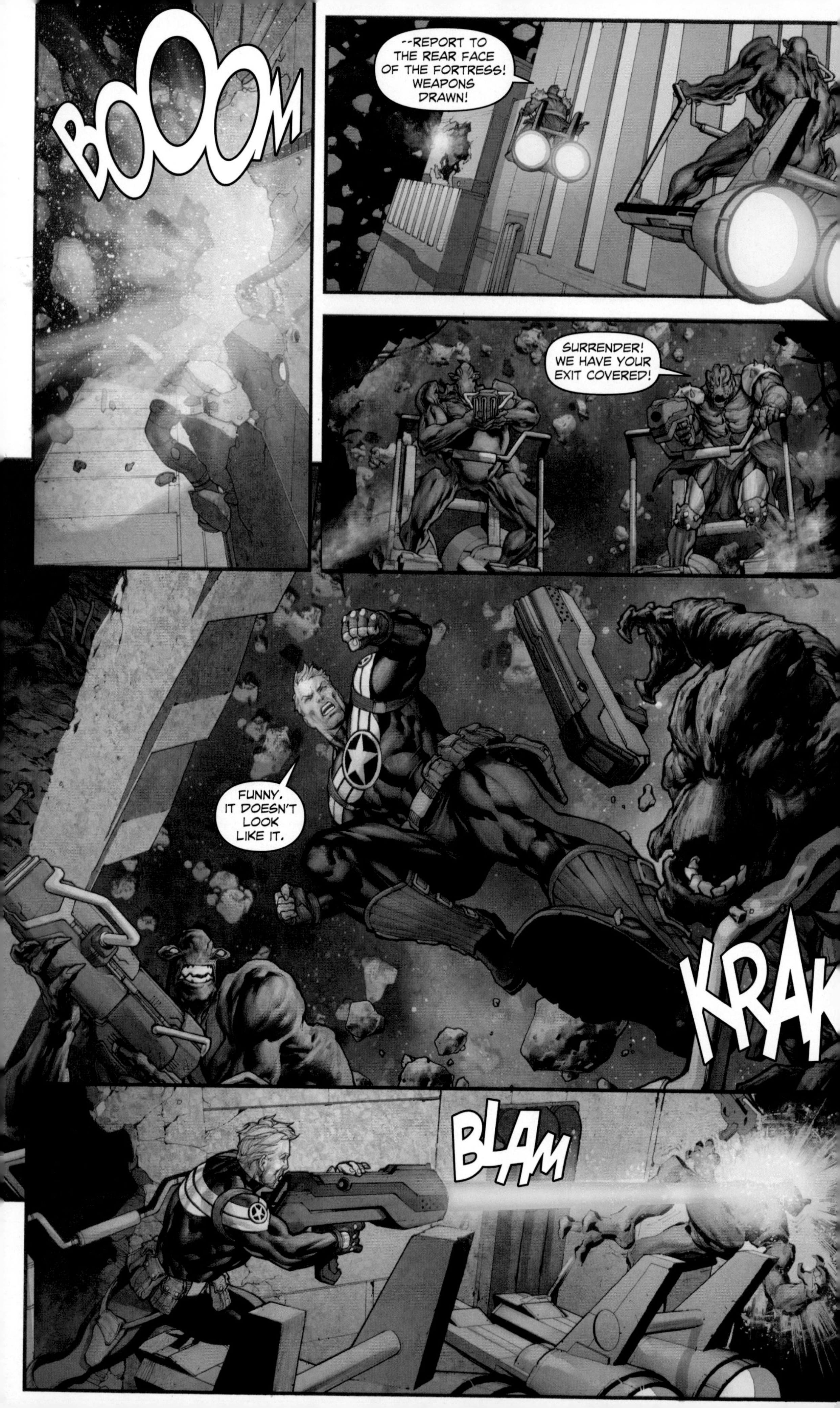
BOOOM
--REPORT TO THE REAR FACE OF THE FORTRESS! WEAPONS DRAWN!
SURRENDER! WE HAVE YOUR EXIT COVERED!
FUNNY. IT DOESN'T LOOK LIKE IT.
KRAK
BLAM

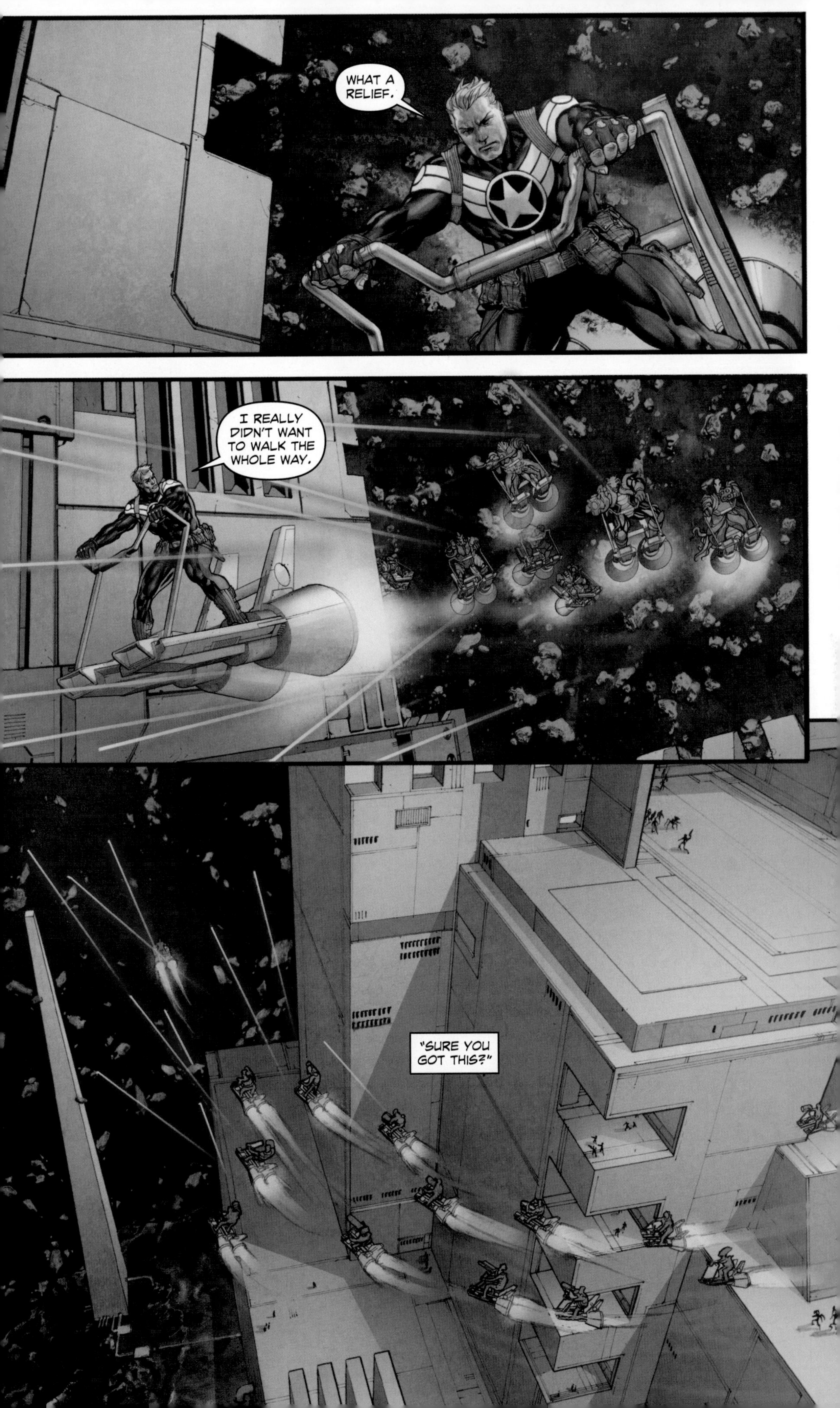

WHAT A RELIEF.
I REALLY DIDN'T WANT TO WALK THE WHOLE WAY.
"SURE YOU GOT THIS?"

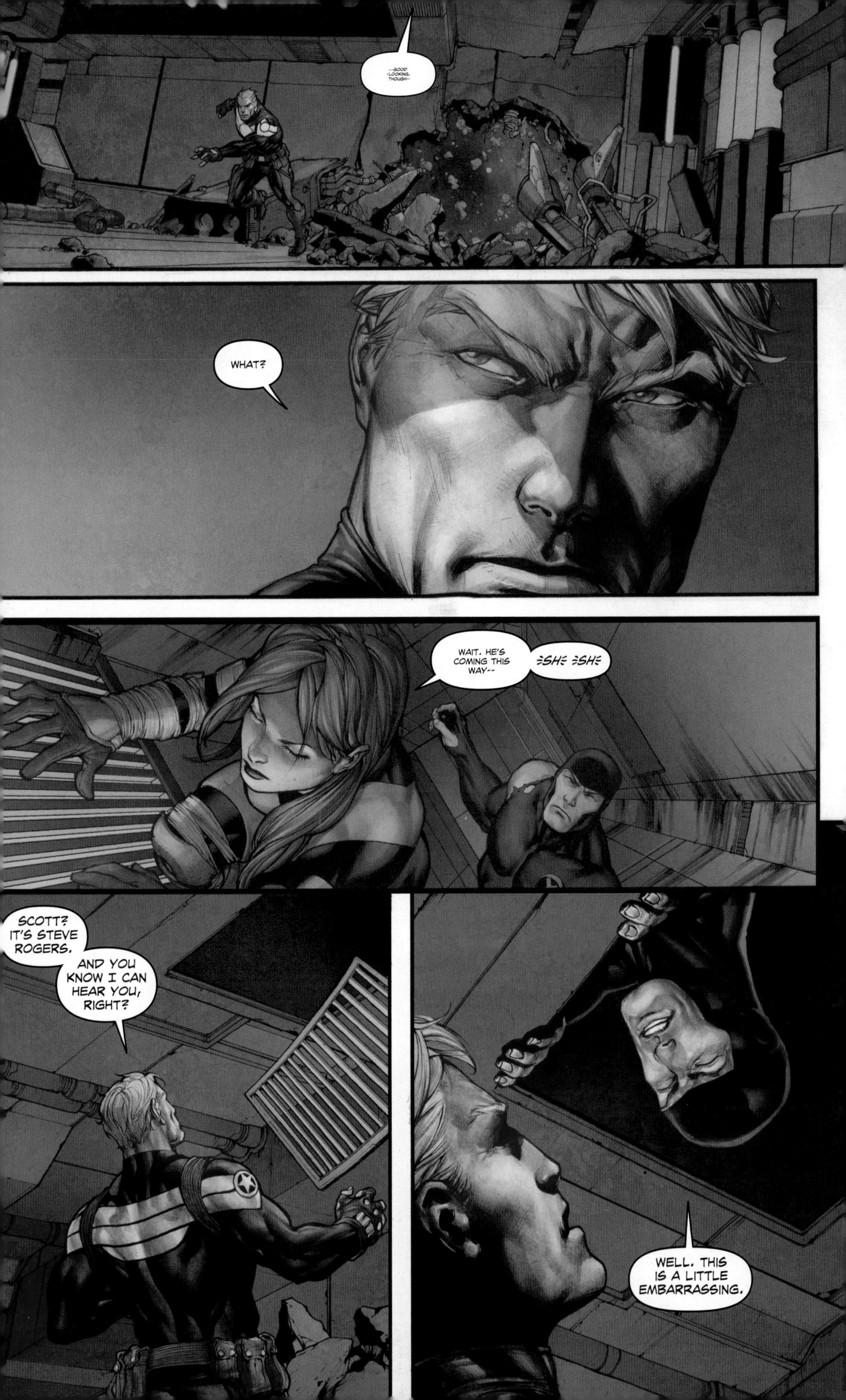
--GOOD -LOOKING, THOUGH--
WHAT?
WAIT. HE'S COMING THIS WAY--
≈SH≈ ≈SH≈
SCOTT? IT'S STEVE ROGERS.
AND YOU KNOW I CAN HEAR YOU, RIGHT?
WELL. THIS IS A LITTLE EMBARRASSING.

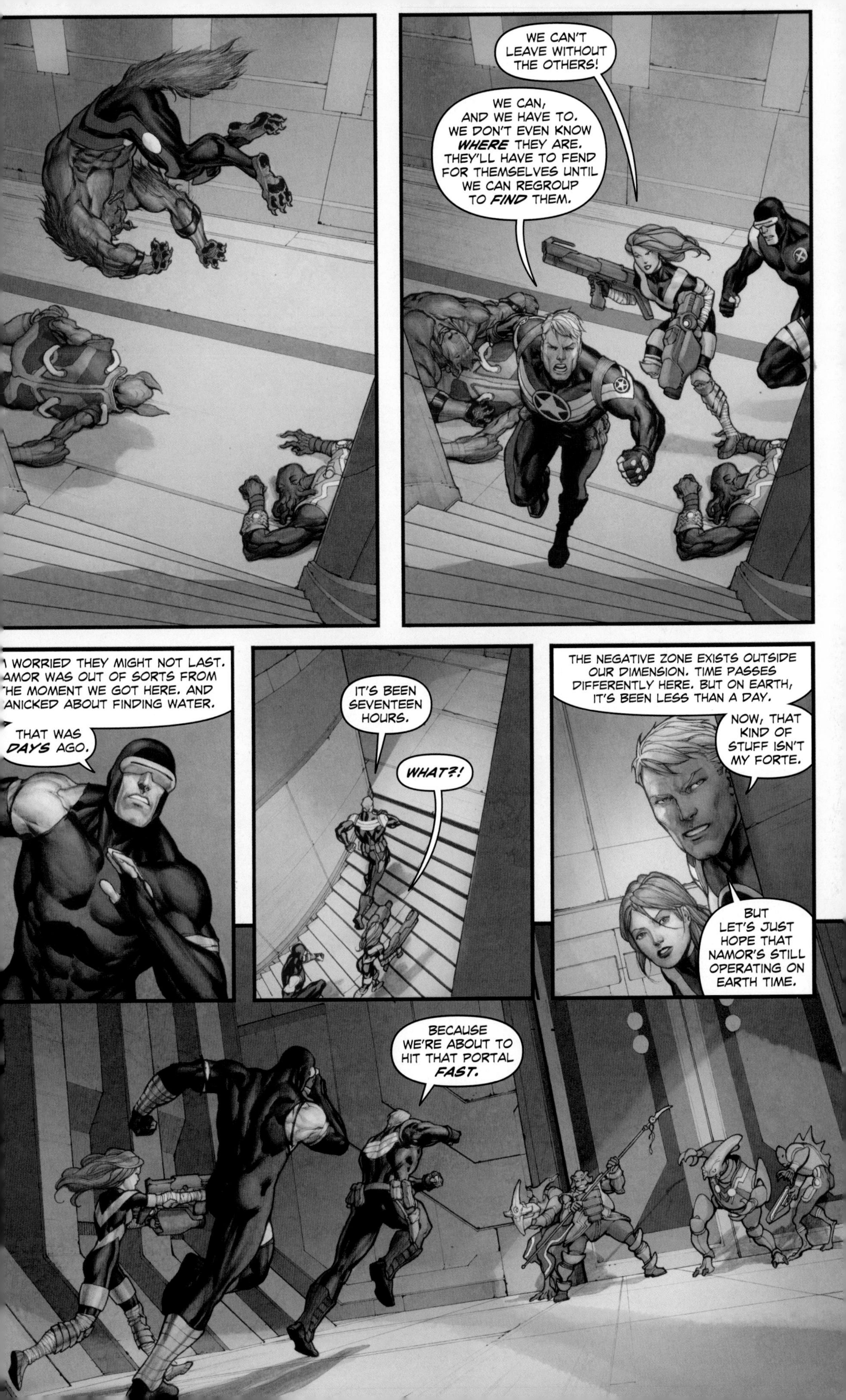

WE CAN'T LEAVE WITHOUT THE OTHERS!
WE CAN, AND WE HAVE TO. WE DON'T EVEN KNOW *WHERE* THEY ARE. THEY'LL HAVE TO FEND FOR THEMSELVES UNTIL WE CAN REGROUP TO *FIND* THEM.
WORRIED THEY MIGHT NOT LAST. AMOR WAS OUT OF SORTS FROM THE MOMENT WE GOT HERE. AND ANICKED ABOUT FINDING WATER.
THAT WAS *DAYS* AGO.
IT'S BEEN SEVENTEEN HOURS.
WHAT?!
THE NEGATIVE ZONE EXISTS OUTSIDE OUR DIMENSION. TIME PASSES DIFFERENTLY HERE. BUT ON EARTH, IT'S BEEN LESS THAN A DAY.
NOW, THAT KIND OF STUFF ISN'T MY FORTE.
BUT LET'S JUST HOPE THAT NAMOR'S STILL OPERATING ON EARTH TIME.
BECAUSE WE'RE ABOUT TO HIT THAT PORTAL *FAST*.

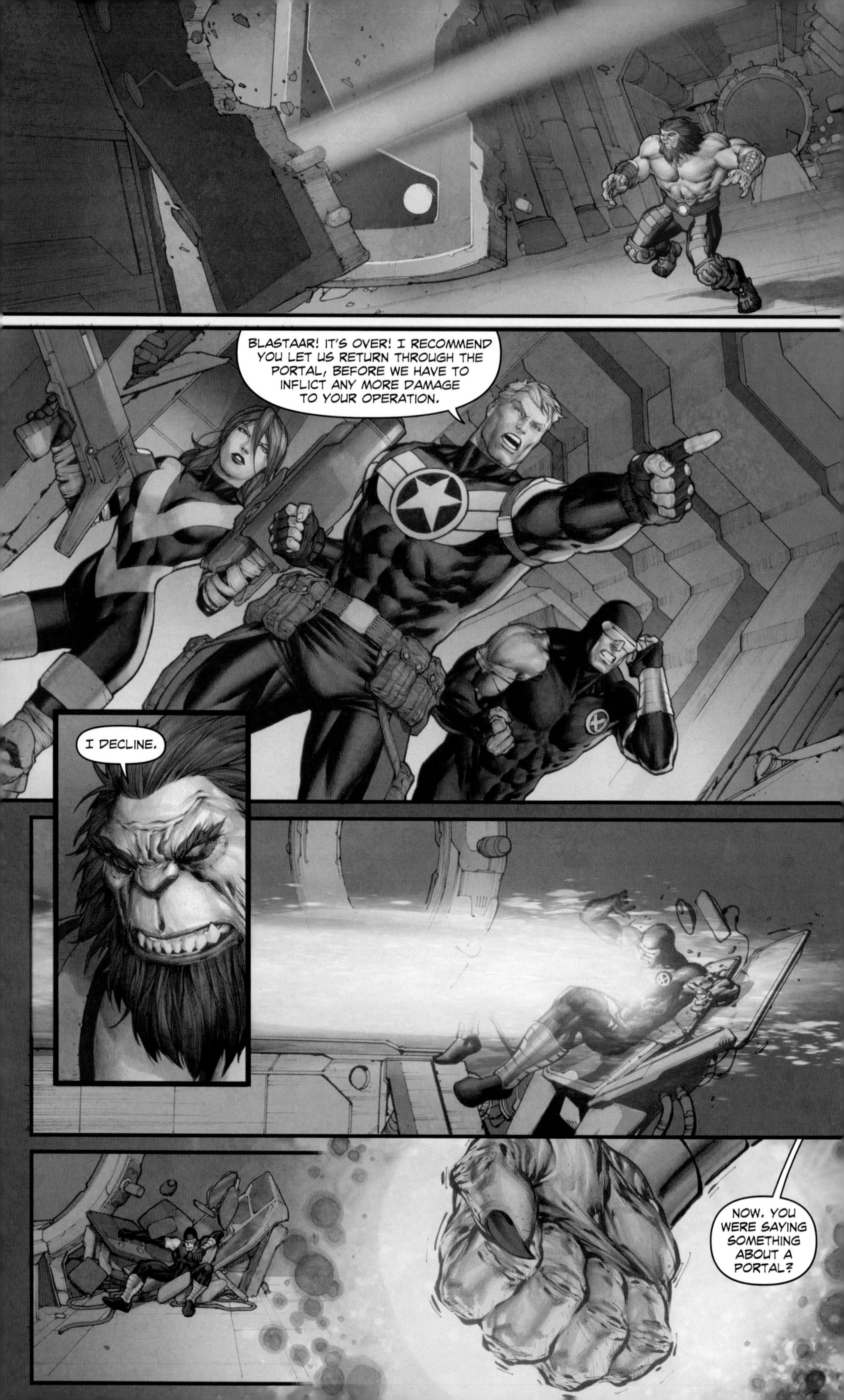
BLASTAAR! IT'S OVER! I RECOMMEND YOU LET US RETURN THROUGH THE PORTAL, BEFORE WE HAVE TO INFLICT ANY MORE DAMAGE TO YOUR OPERATION.
I DECLINE.
NOW. YOU WERE SAYING SOMETHING ABOUT A PORTAL?

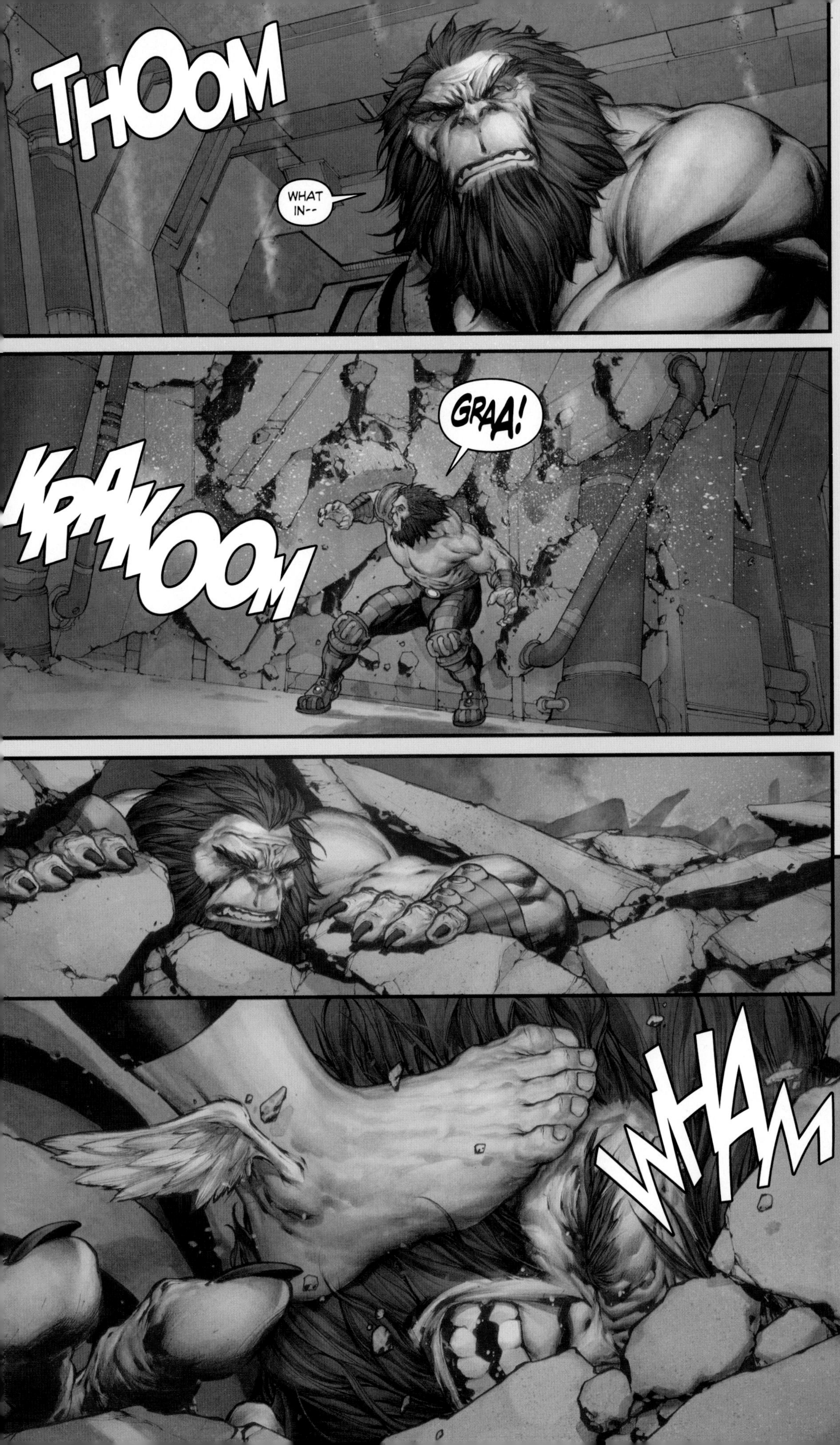
THOOM
WHAT IN--
GRAA!
KRAKOOM
WHAM

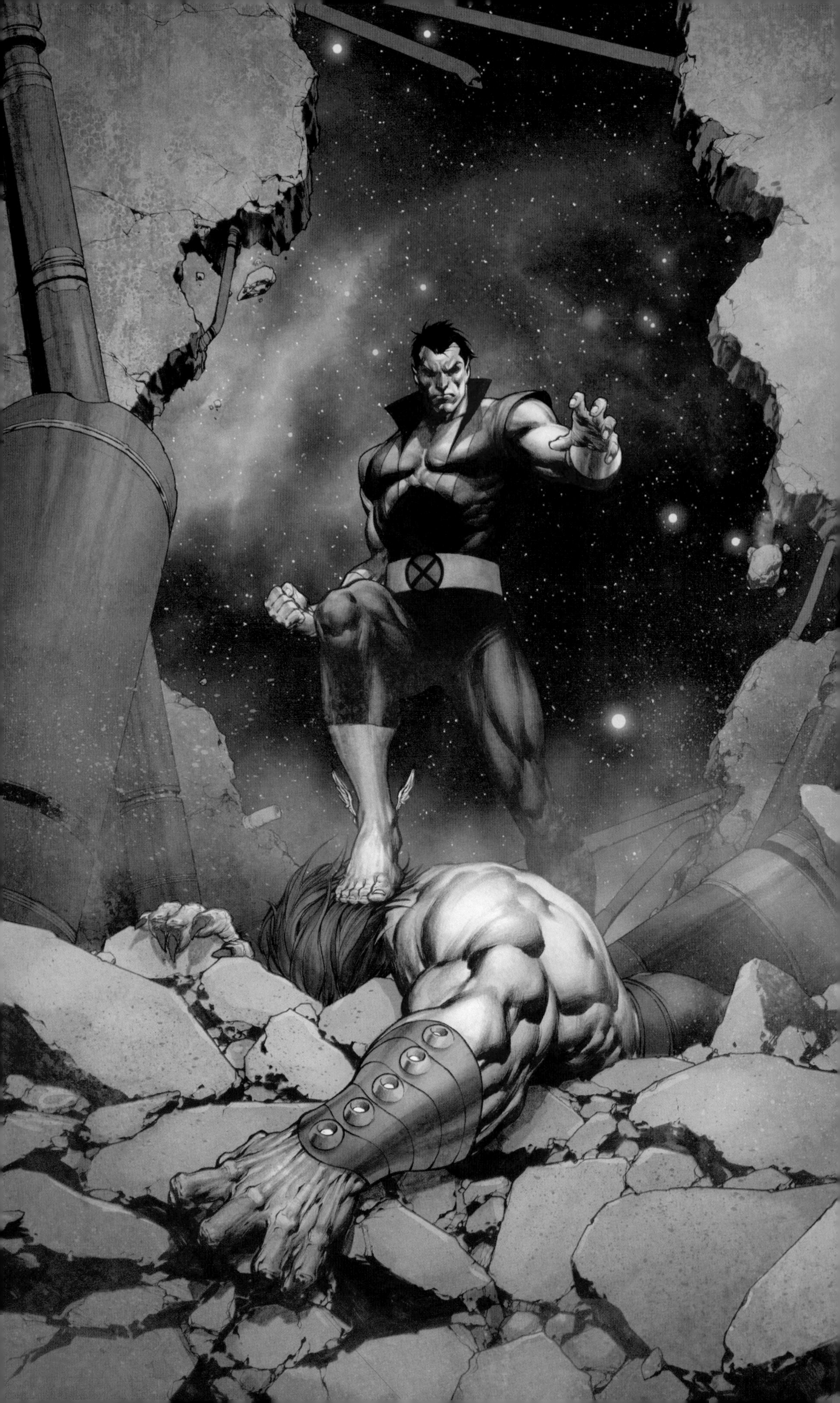

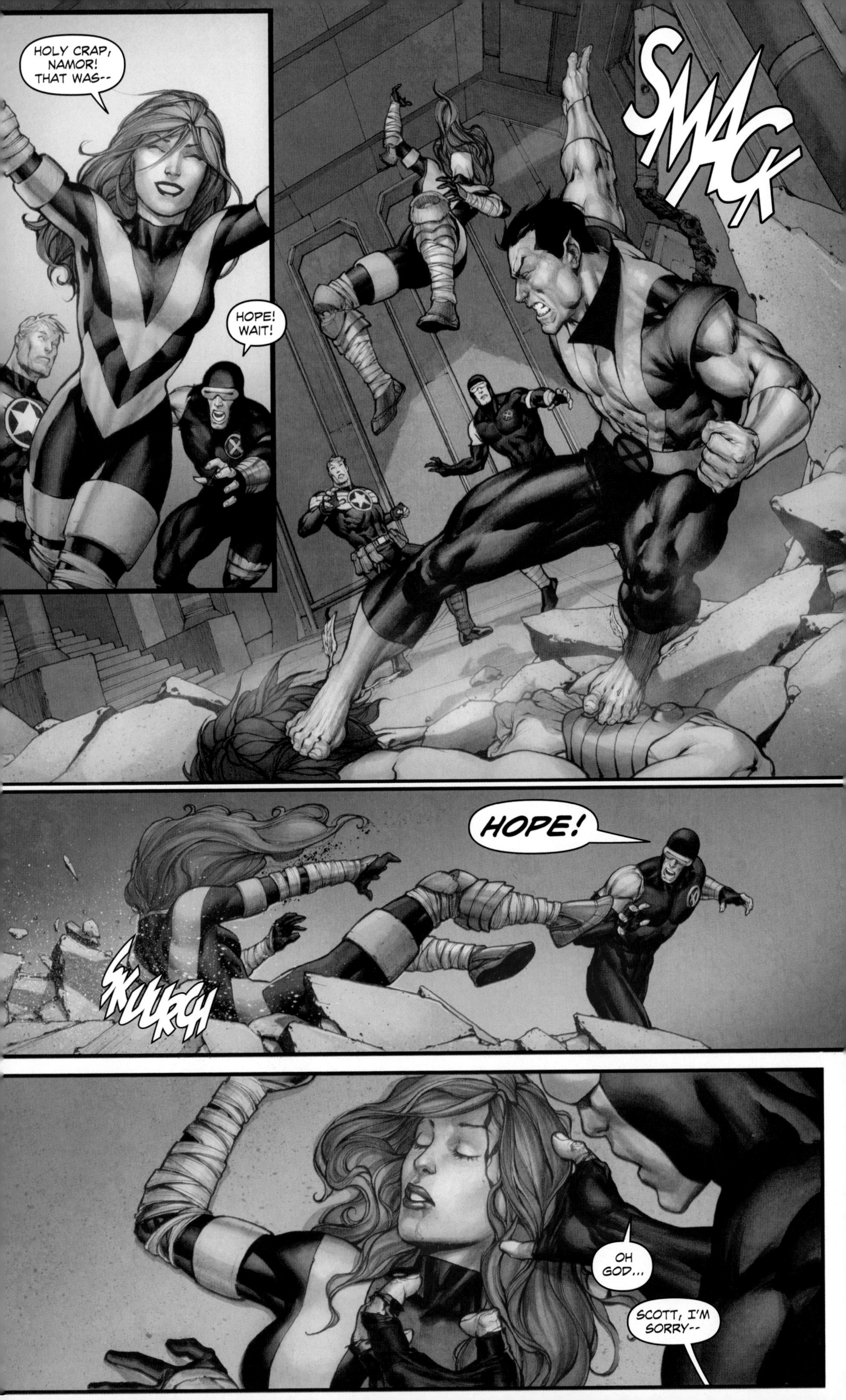
HOLY CRAP, NAMOR! THAT WAS--
HOPE! WAIT!
SMACK
HOPE!
SKLUURCH
OH GOD...
SCOTT, I'M SORRY--

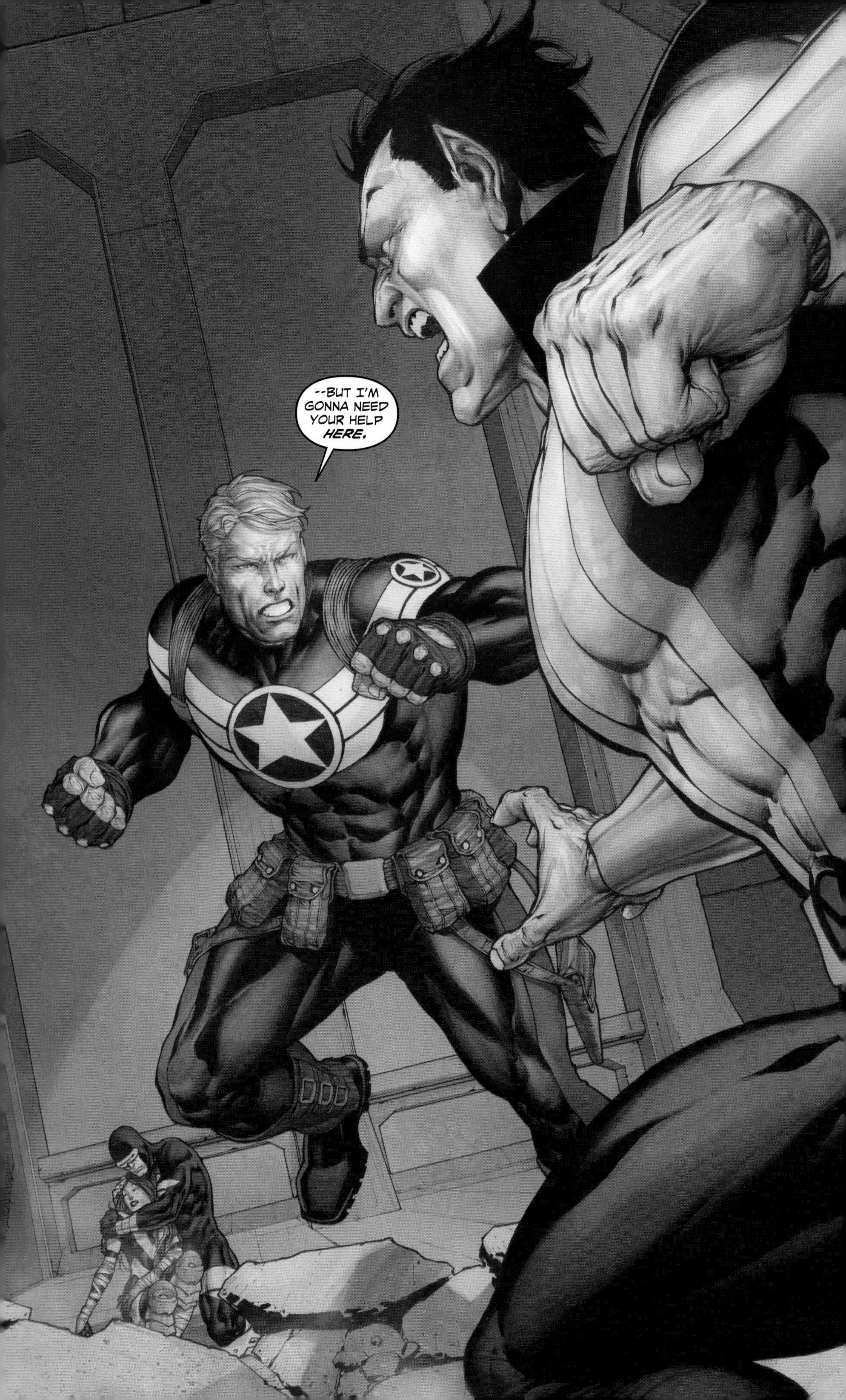
--BUT I'M GONNA NEED YOUR HELP *HERE.*

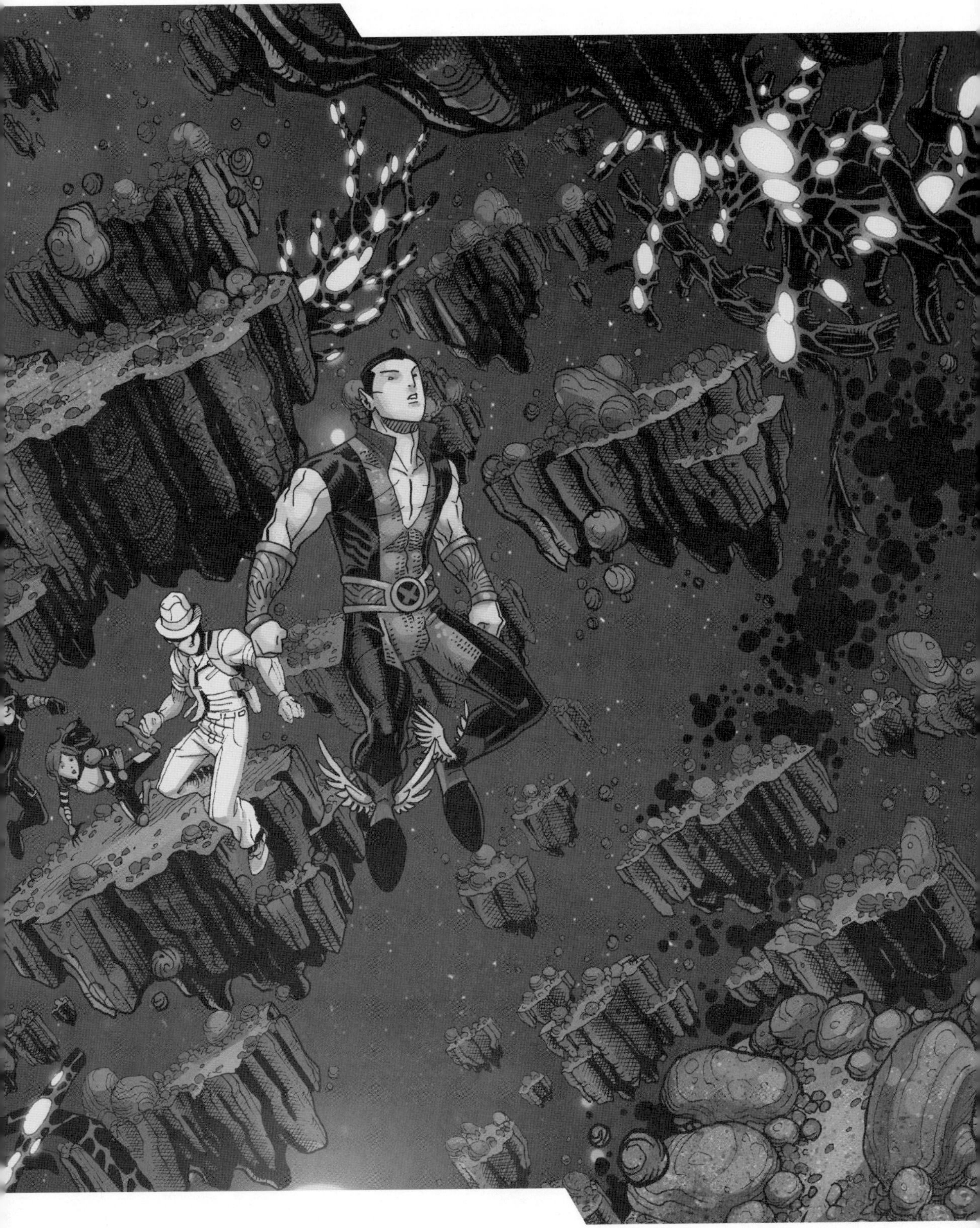

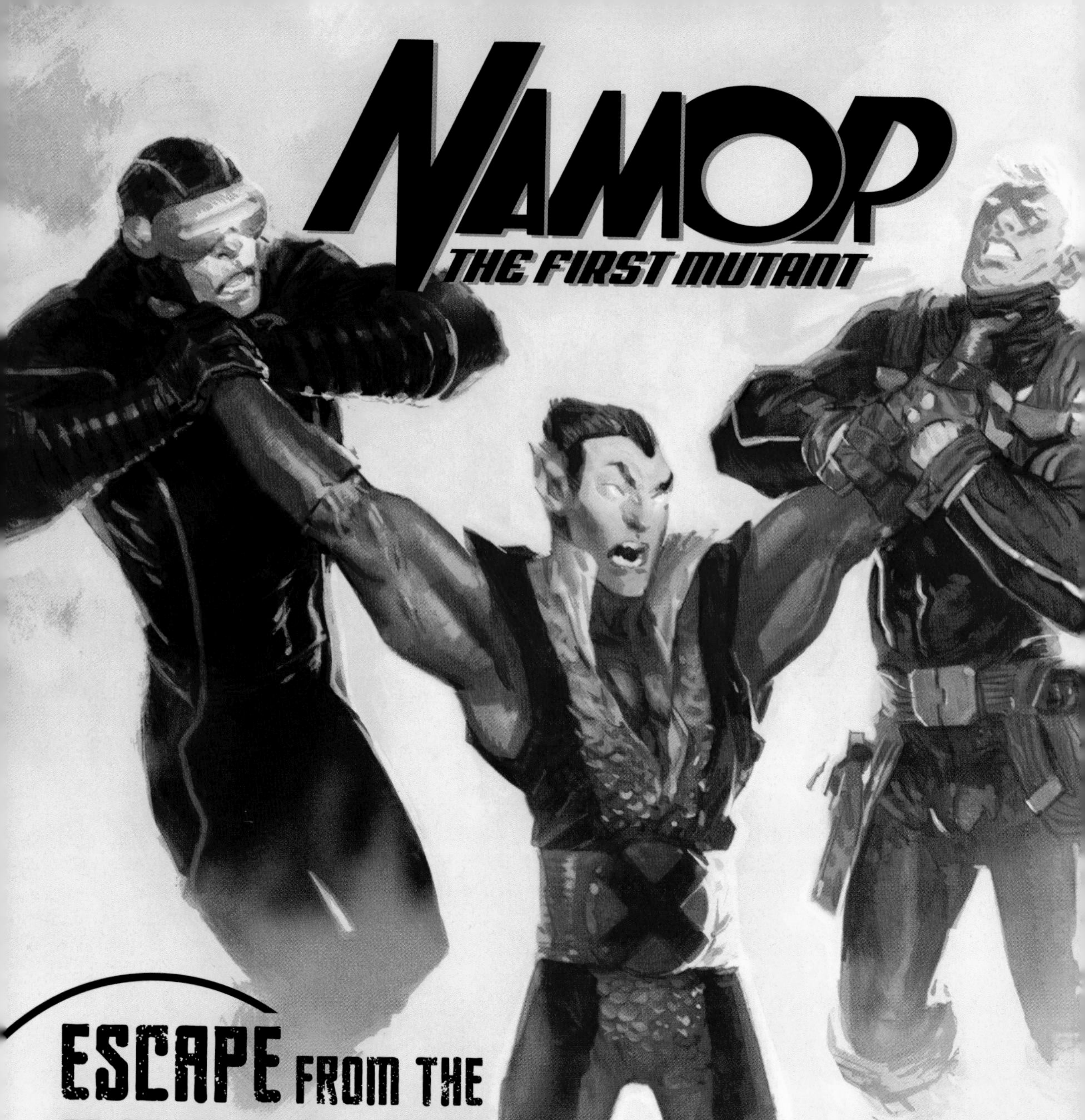
NAMOR
THE FIRST MUTANT
ESCAPE FROM THE
NEGATIVE
ZONE
PART THREE

ANNUAL #01 2011

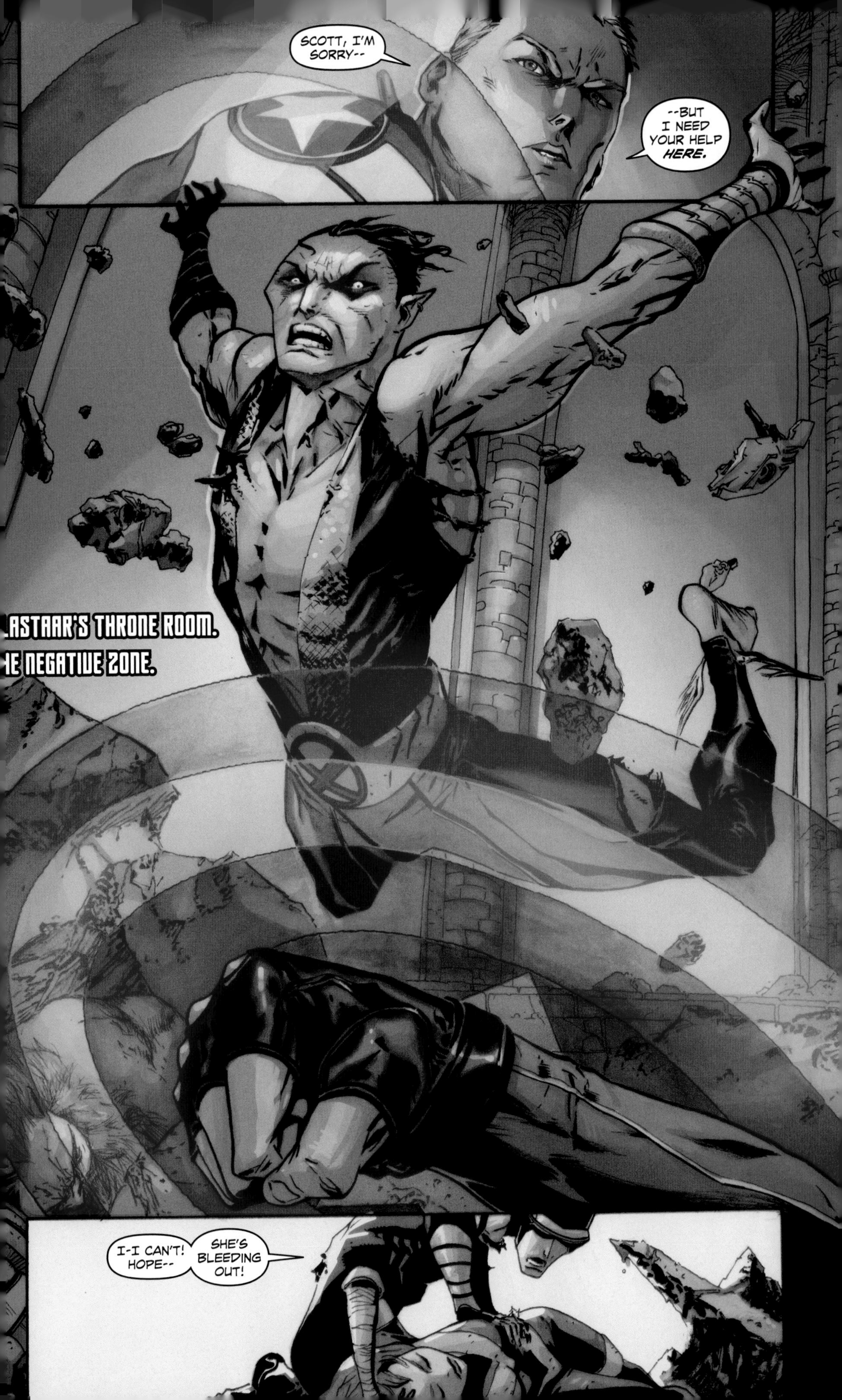
SCOTT, I'M SORRY--
--BUT I NEED YOUR HELP *HERE.*
LASTAAR'S THRONE ROOM.
IE NEGATIVE ZONE.
I-I CAN'T! HOPE--
SHE'S BLEEDING OUT!

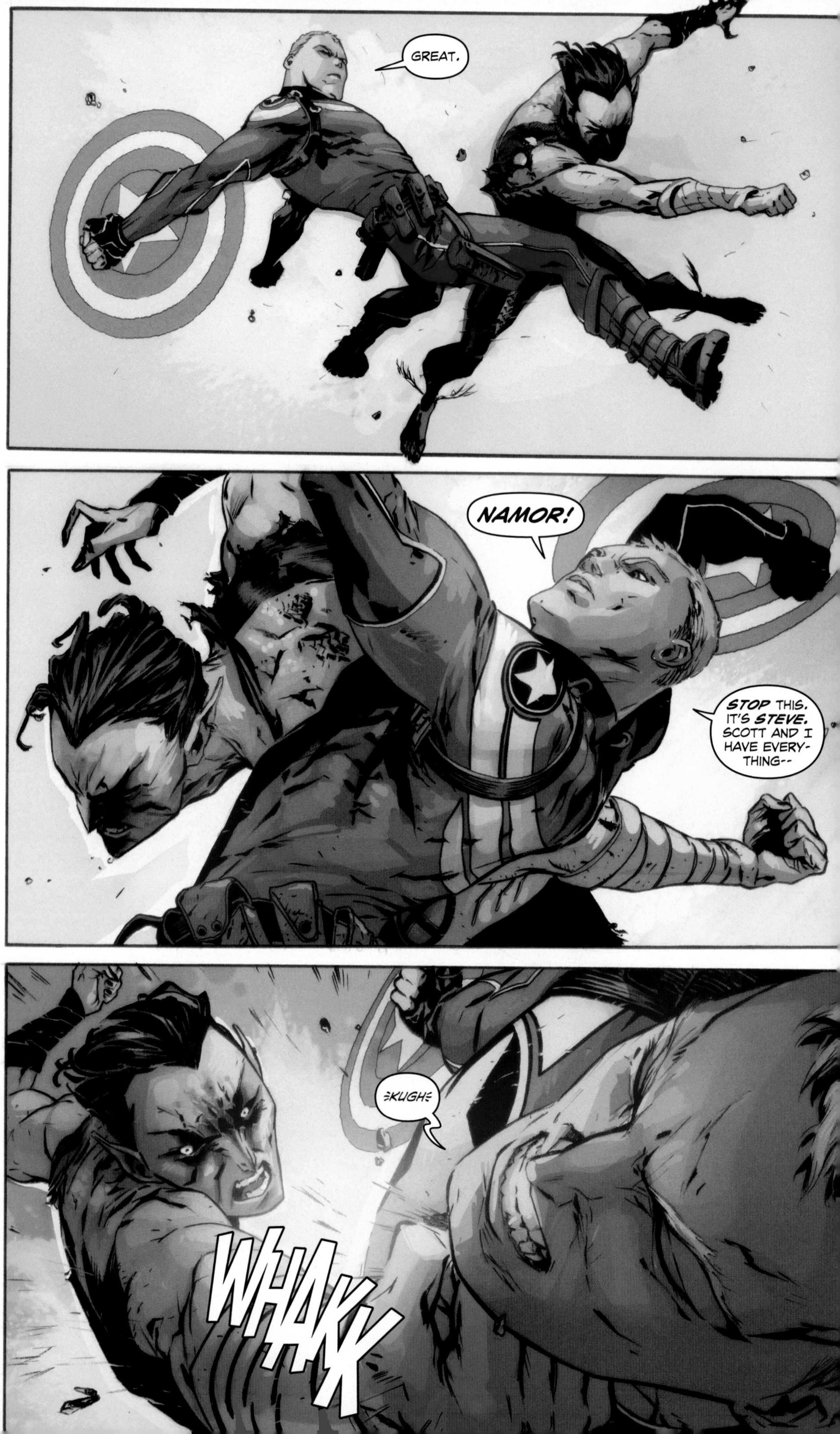
GREAT.
NAMOR!
STOP THIS. IT'S STEVE. SCOTT AND I HAVE EVERYTHING--
KUGH
WHAKK

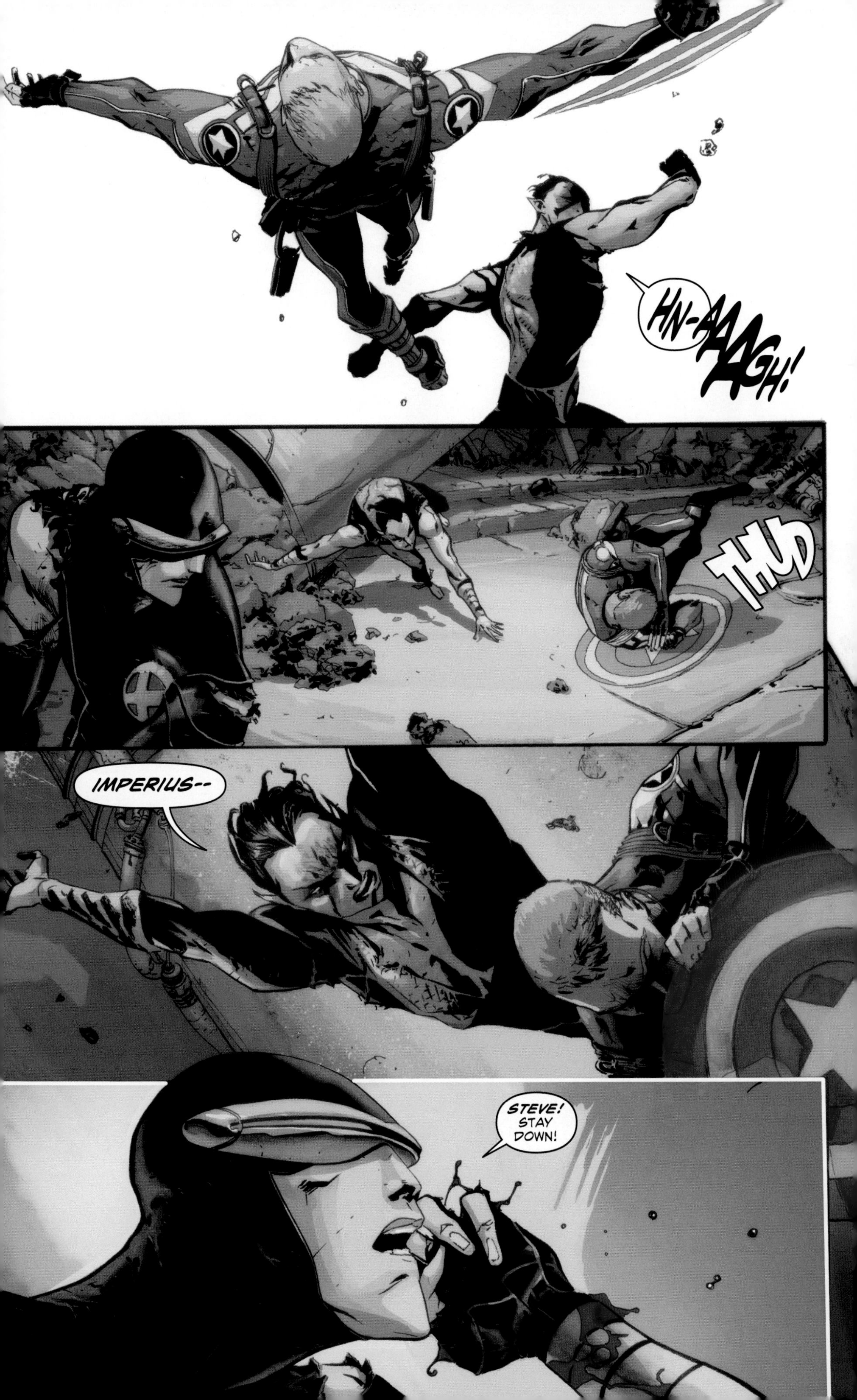
HN-AAAGH!
THUD
IMPERIUS--
STEVE! STAY DOWN!

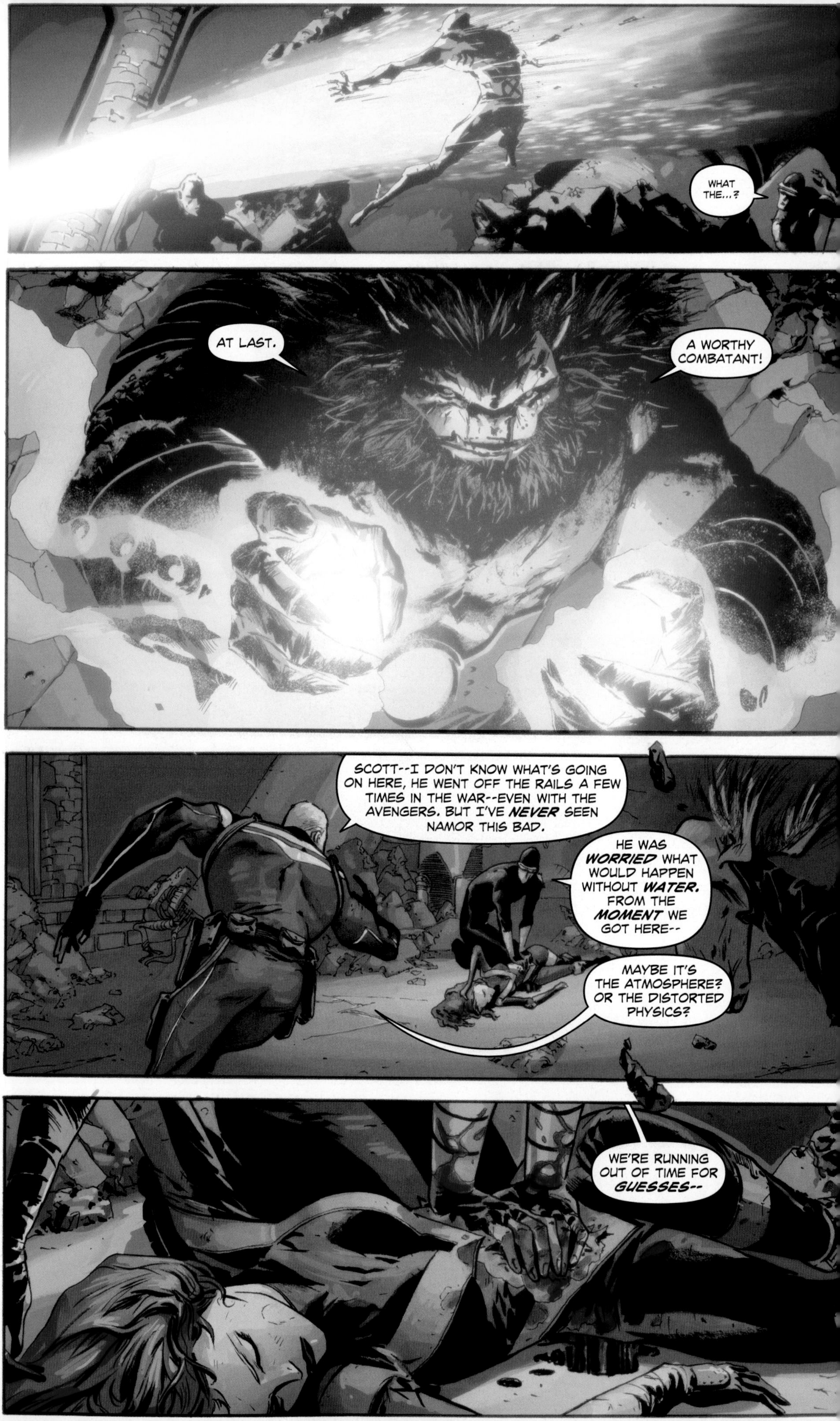
WHAT THE...?
AT LAST.
A WORTHY COMBATANT!
SCOTT--I DON'T KNOW WHAT'S GOING ON HERE, HE WENT OFF THE RAILS A FEW TIMES IN THE WAR--EVEN WITH THE AVENGERS. BUT I'VE NEVER SEEN NAMOR THIS BAD.
HE WAS WORRIED WHAT WOULD HAPPEN WITHOUT WATER. FROM THE MOMENT WE GOT HERE--
MAYBE IT'S THE ATMOSPHERE? OR THE DISTORTED PHYSICS?
WE'RE RUNNING OUT OF TIME FOR GUESSES--

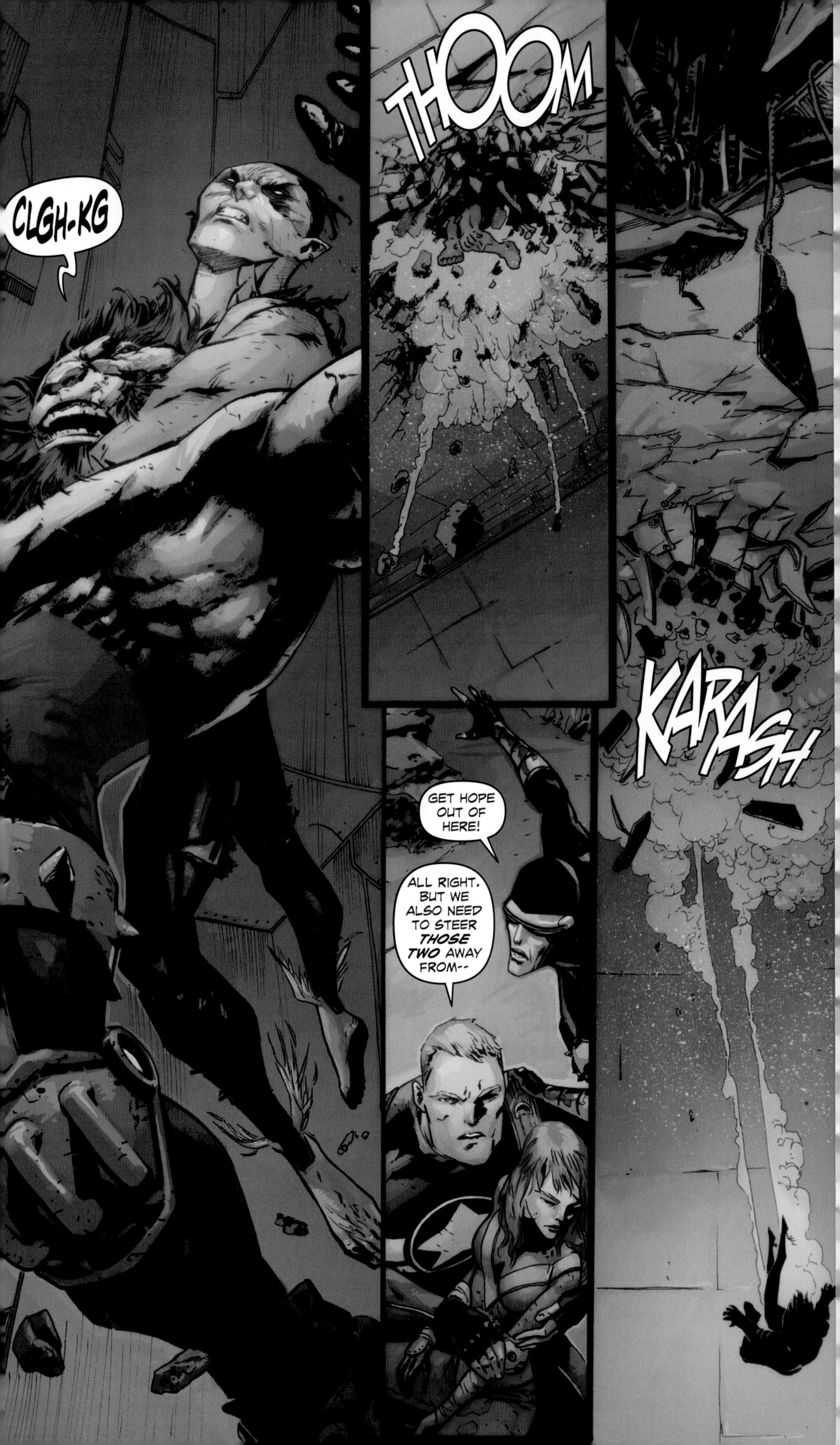
CLGH-KG
THOOM
KARASH
GET HOPE OUT OF HERE!
ALL RIGHT. BUT WE ALSO NEED TO STEER *THOSE TWO* AWAY FROM--

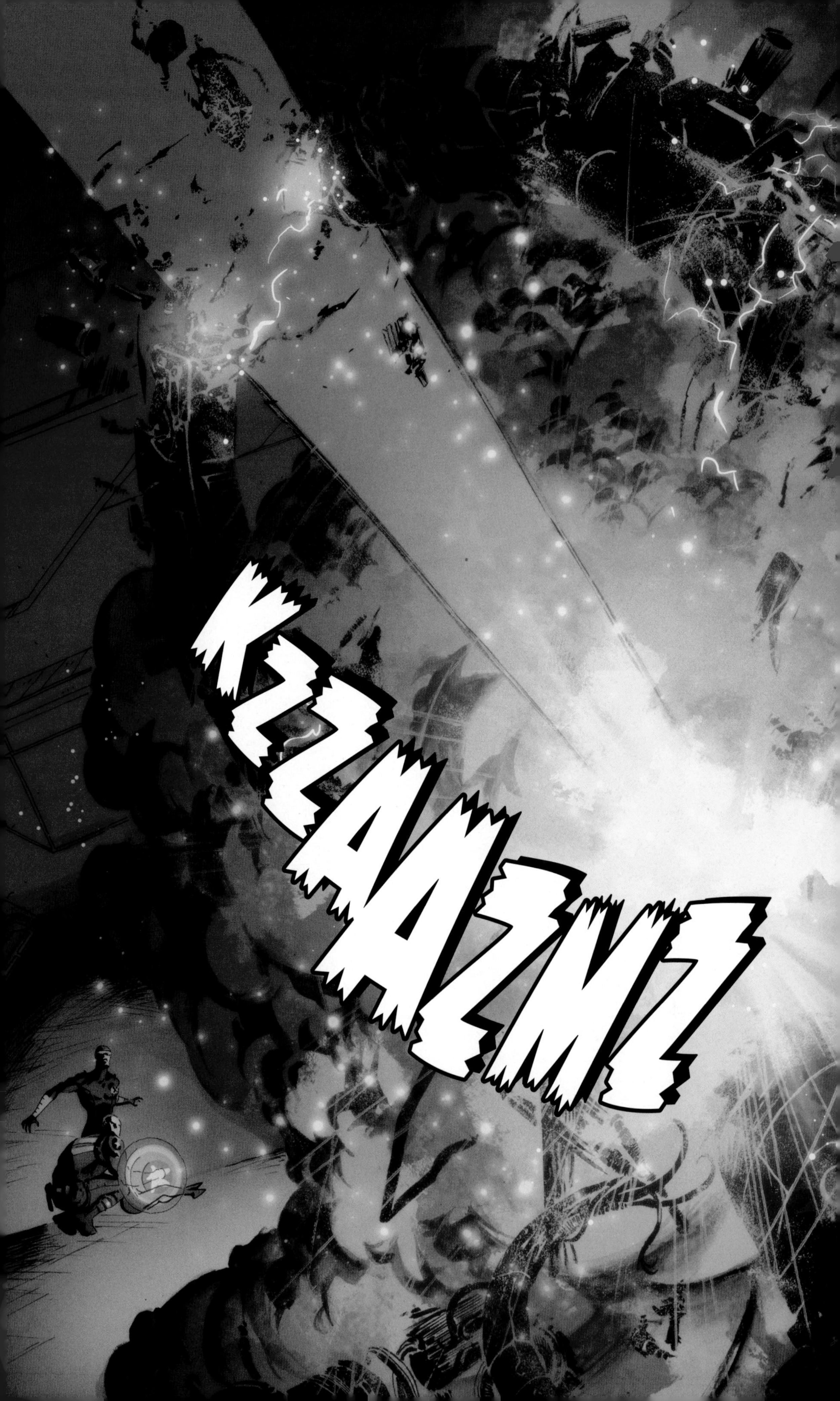
KZZAAZM!

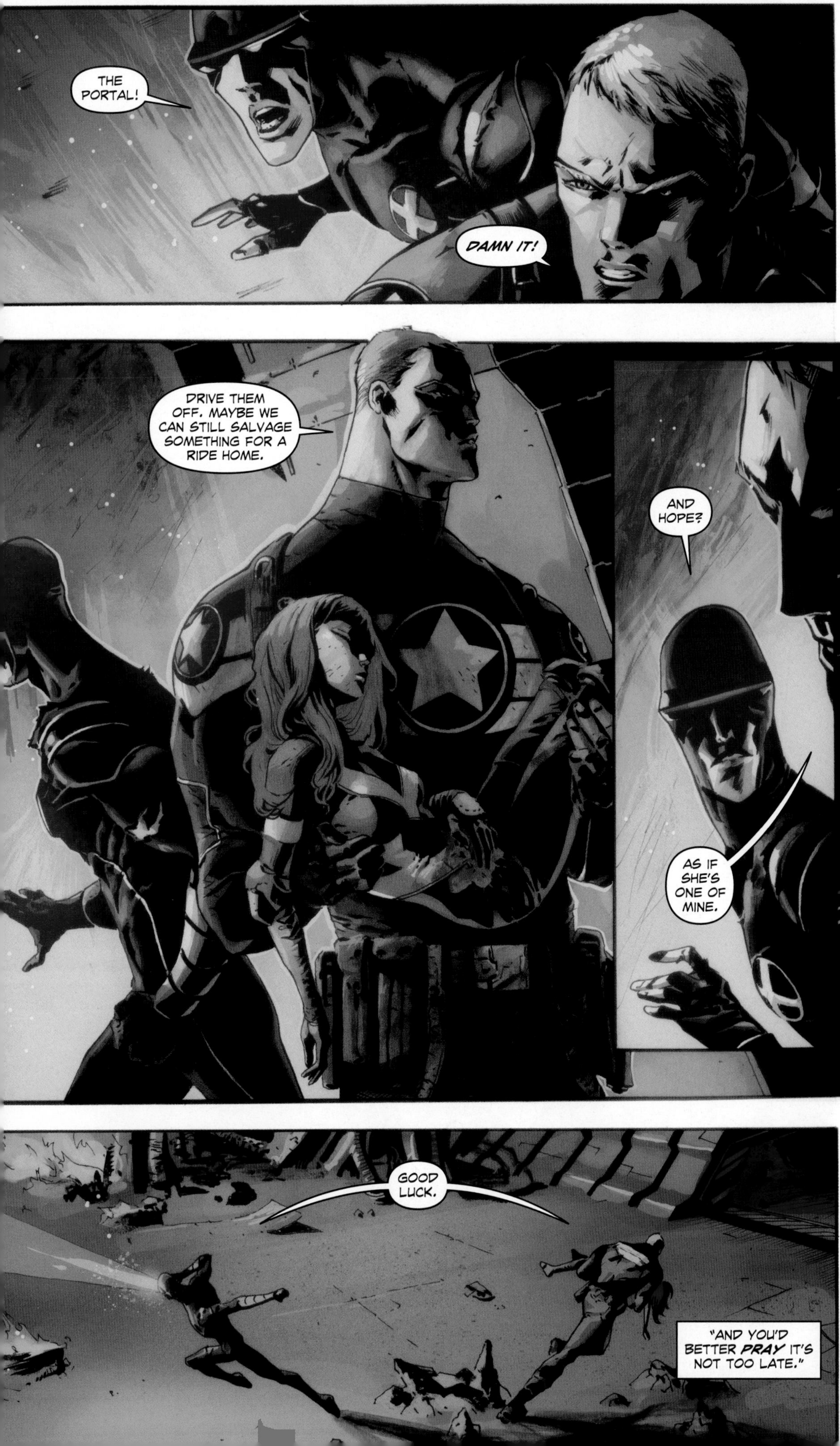
THE PORTAL!
DAMN IT!
DRIVE THEM OFF. MAYBE WE CAN STILL SALVAGE SOMETHING FOR A RIDE HOME.
AND HOPE?
AS IF SHE'S ONE OF MINE.
GOOD LUCK.
"AND YOU'D BETTER PRAY IT'S NOT TOO LATE."

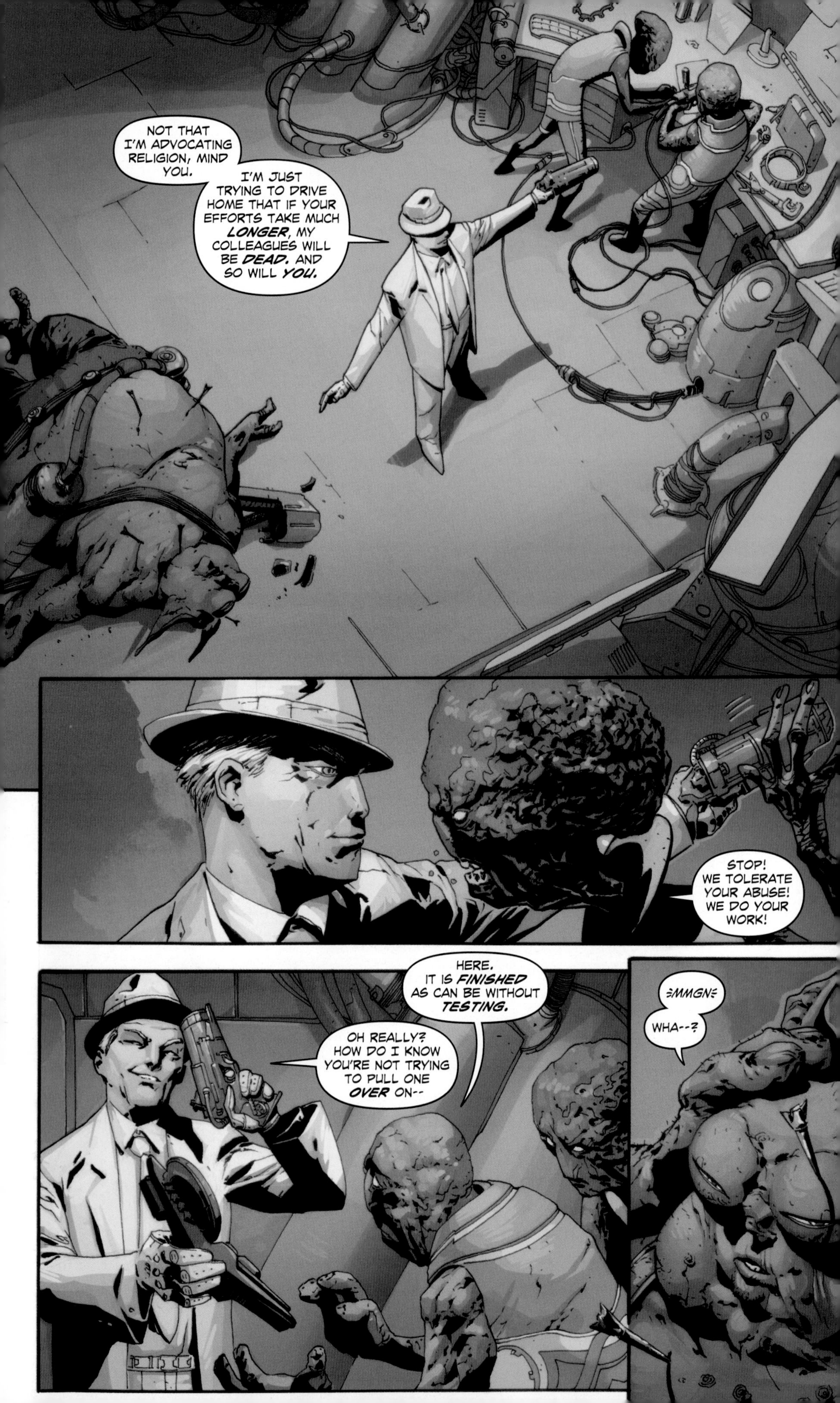
NOT THAT I'M ADVOCATING RELIGION, MIND YOU.
I'M JUST TRYING TO DRIVE HOME THAT IF YOUR EFFORTS TAKE MUCH *LONGER*, MY COLLEAGUES WILL BE *DEAD*. AND SO WILL *YOU*.
STOP! WE TOLERATE YOUR ABUSE! WE DO YOUR WORK!
HERE. IT IS *FINISHED* AS CAN BE WITHOUT *TESTING*.
OH REALLY? HOW DO I KNOW YOU'RE NOT TRYING TO PULL ONE *OVER* ON--
MMGN
WHA--?

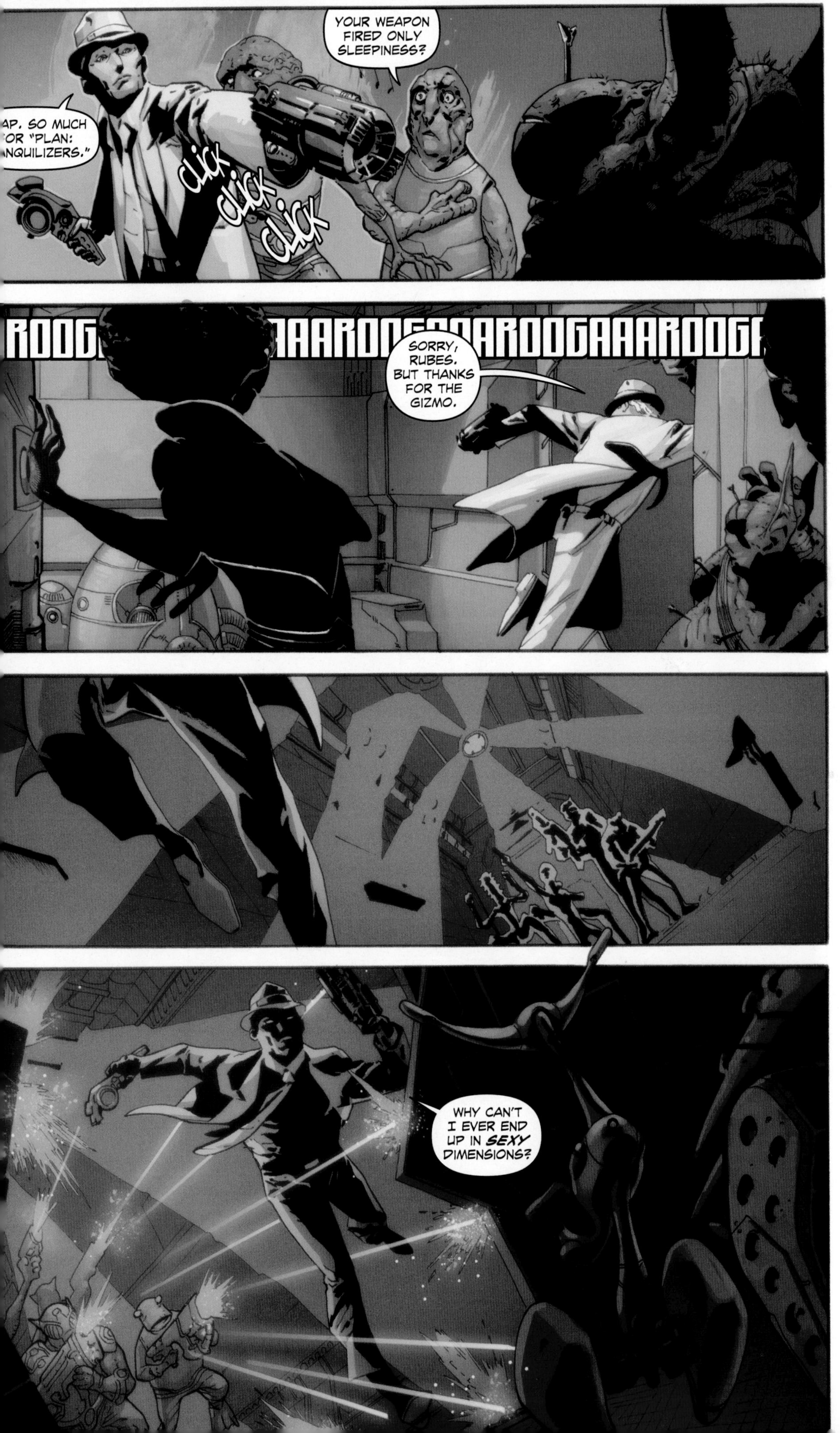

YOUR WEAPON FIRED ONLY SLEEPINESS?
AP. SO MUCH FOR "PLAN: ANQUILIZERS."
CLICK CLICK CLICK
ROOG AAARO AAROOGAAAROOG
SORRY, RUBES. BUT THANKS FOR THE GIZMO.
WHY CAN'T I EVER END UP IN *SEXY* DIMENSIONS?

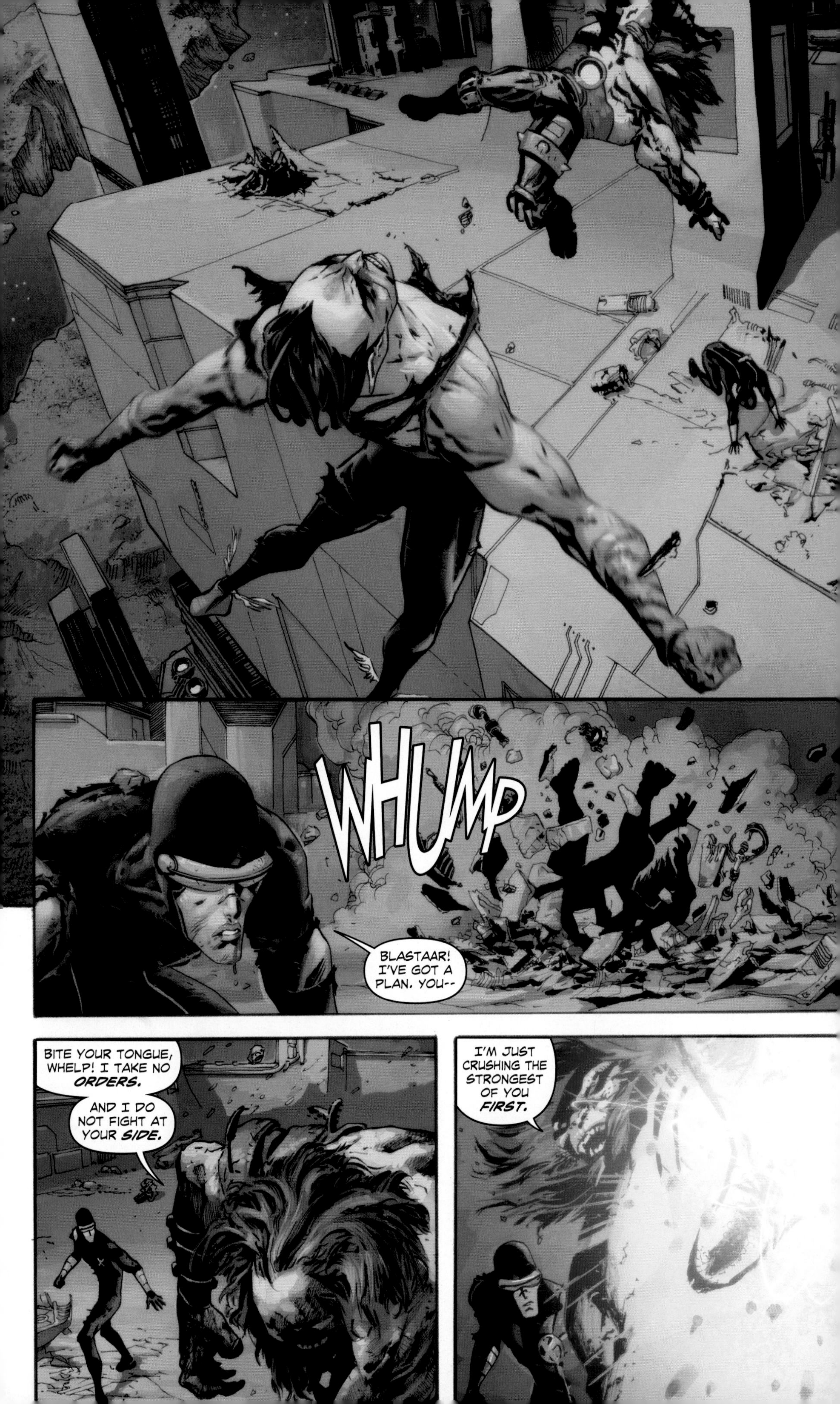
WHUMP
BLASTAAR! I'VE GOT A PLAN. YOU--
BITE YOUR TONGUE, WHELP! I TAKE NO ORDERS.
AND I DO NOT FIGHT AT YOUR SIDE.
I'M JUST CRUSHING THE STRONGEST OF YOU FIRST.

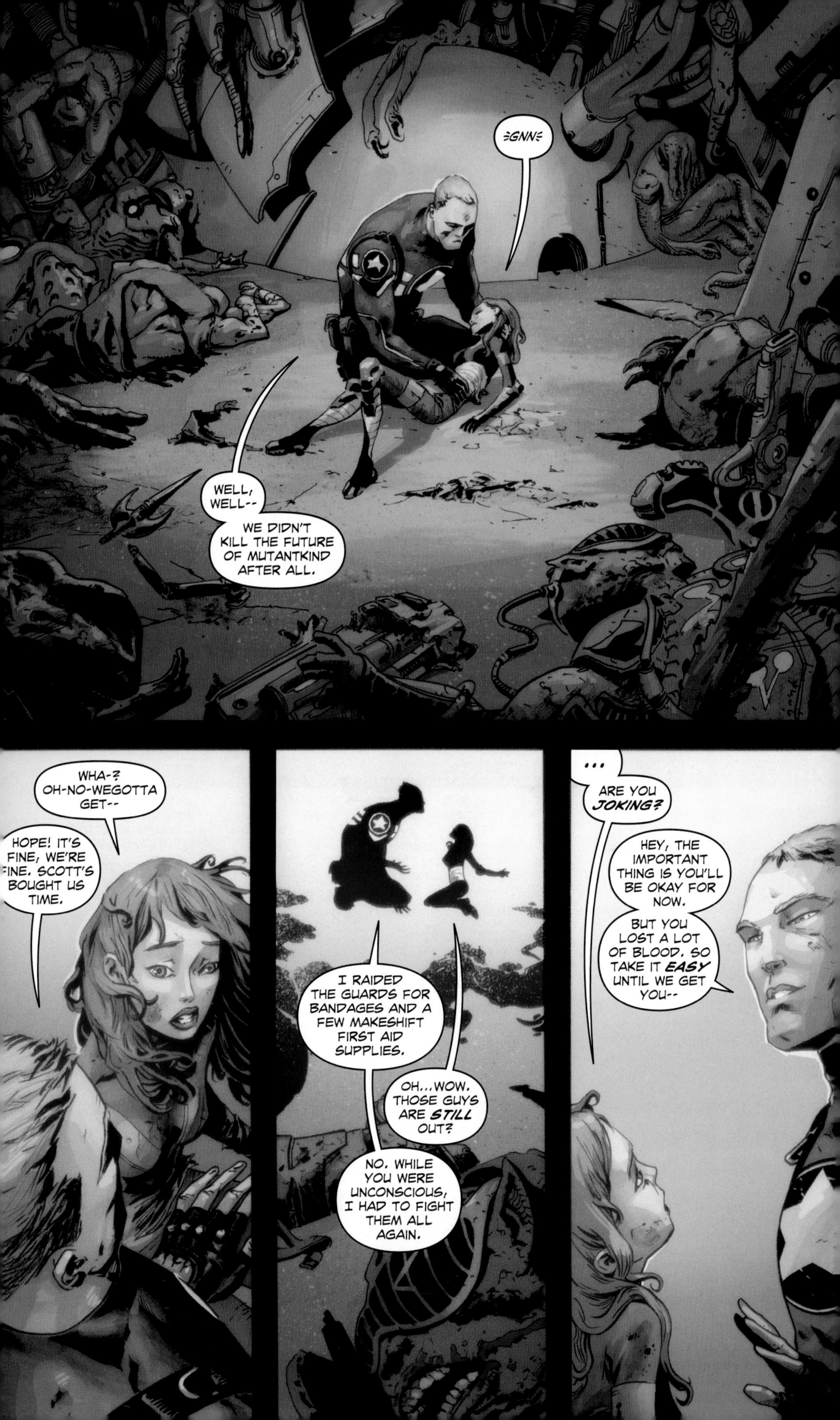

≡GNN≡
WELL, WELL--
WE DIDN'T KILL THE FUTURE OF MUTANTKIND AFTER ALL.
WHA-? OH-NO-WEGOTTA GET--
HOPE! IT'S FINE, WE'RE FINE. SCOTT'S BOUGHT US TIME.
I RAIDED THE GUARDS FOR BANDAGES AND A FEW MAKESHIFT FIRST AID SUPPLIES.
OH...WOW. THOSE GUYS ARE STILL OUT?
NO. WHILE YOU WERE UNCONSCIOUS, I HAD TO FIGHT THEM ALL AGAIN.
...
ARE YOU JOKING?
HEY, THE IMPORTANT THING IS YOU'LL BE OKAY FOR NOW.
BUT YOU LOST A LOT OF BLOOD. SO TAKE IT EASY UNTIL WE GET YOU--

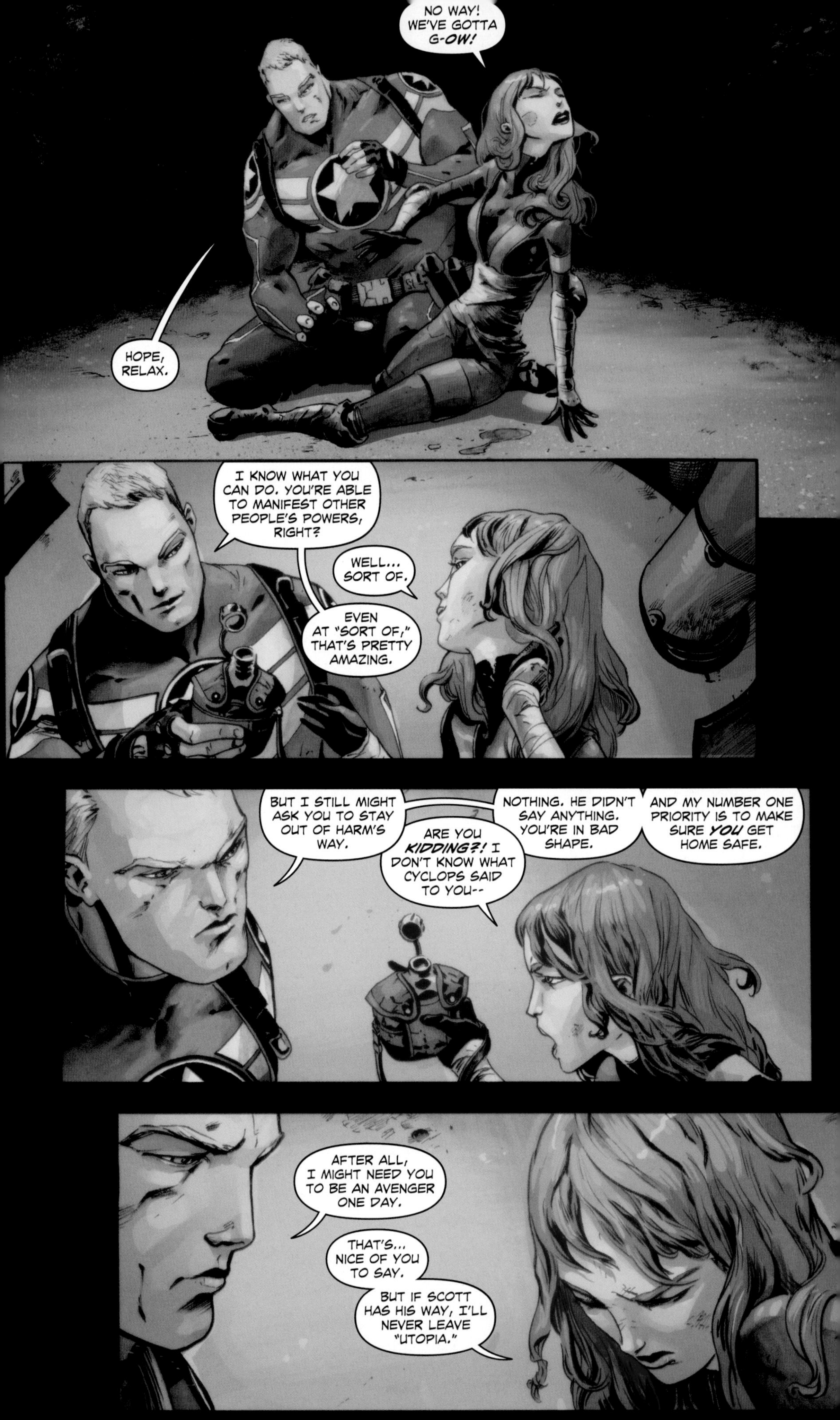
NO WAY! WE'VE GOTTA G-OW!
HOPE, RELAX.
I KNOW WHAT YOU CAN DO. YOU'RE ABLE TO MANIFEST OTHER PEOPLE'S POWERS, RIGHT?
WELL... SORT OF.
EVEN AT "SORT OF," THAT'S PRETTY AMAZING.
BUT I STILL MIGHT ASK YOU TO STAY OUT OF HARM'S WAY.
ARE YOU KIDDING?! I DON'T KNOW WHAT CYCLOPS SAID TO YOU--
NOTHING. HE DIDN'T SAY ANYTHING. YOU'RE IN BAD SHAPE.
AND MY NUMBER ONE PRIORITY IS TO MAKE SURE YOU GET HOME SAFE.
AFTER ALL, I MIGHT NEED YOU TO BE AN AVENGER ONE DAY.
THAT'S... NICE OF YOU TO SAY.
BUT IF SCOTT HAS HIS WAY, I'LL NEVER LEAVE "UTOPIA."

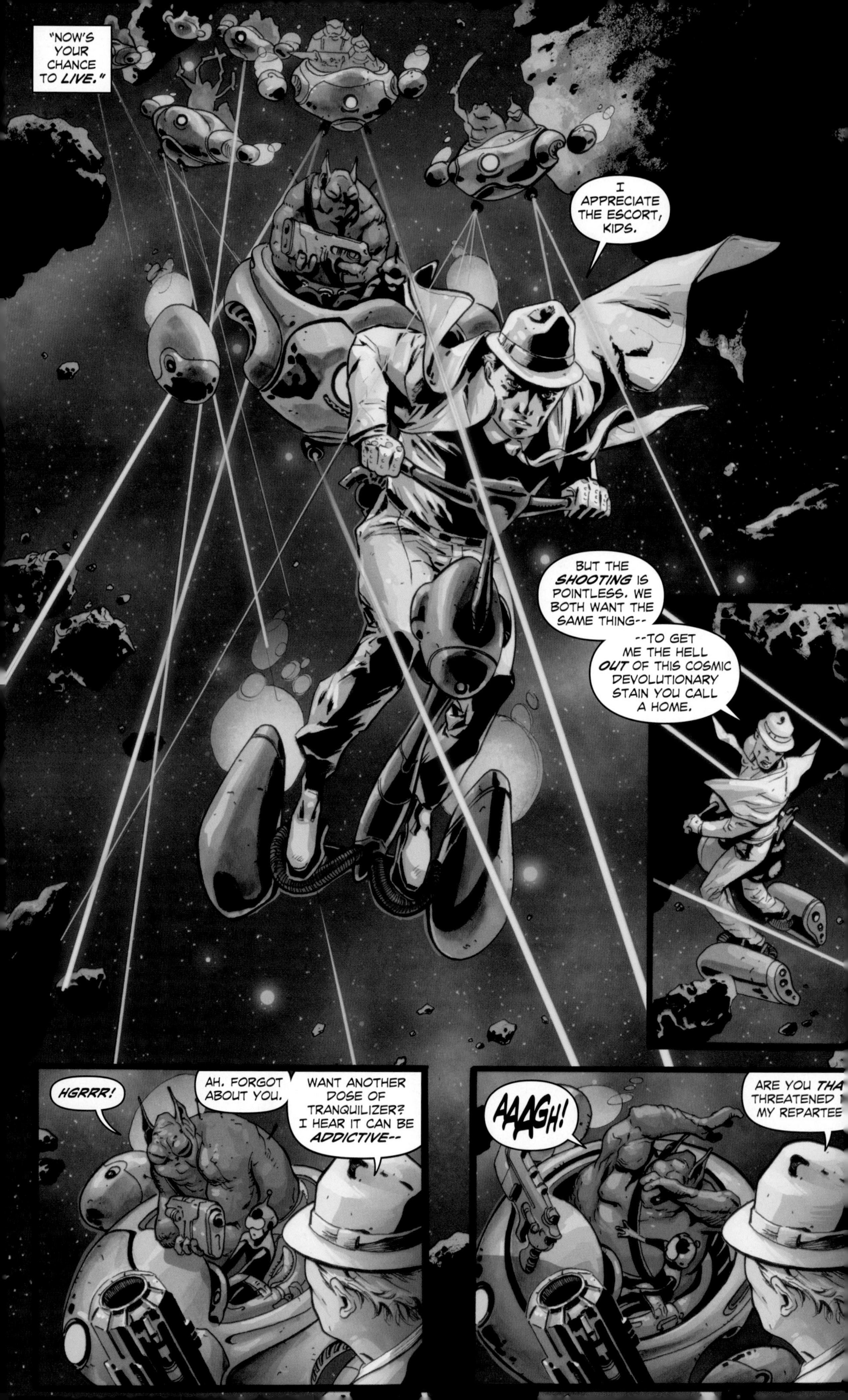
"NOW'S YOUR CHANCE TO LIVE."
I APPRECIATE THE ESCORT, KIDS.
BUT THE SHOOTING IS POINTLESS. WE BOTH WANT THE SAME THING--
--TO GET ME THE HELL OUT OF THIS COSMIC DEVOLUTIONARY STAIN YOU CALL A HOME.
HGRRR!
AH. FORGOT ABOUT YOU.
WANT ANOTHER DOSE OF TRANQUILIZER? I HEAR IT CAN BE ADDICTIVE--
AAAGH!
ARE YOU THA THREATENED MY REPARTEE

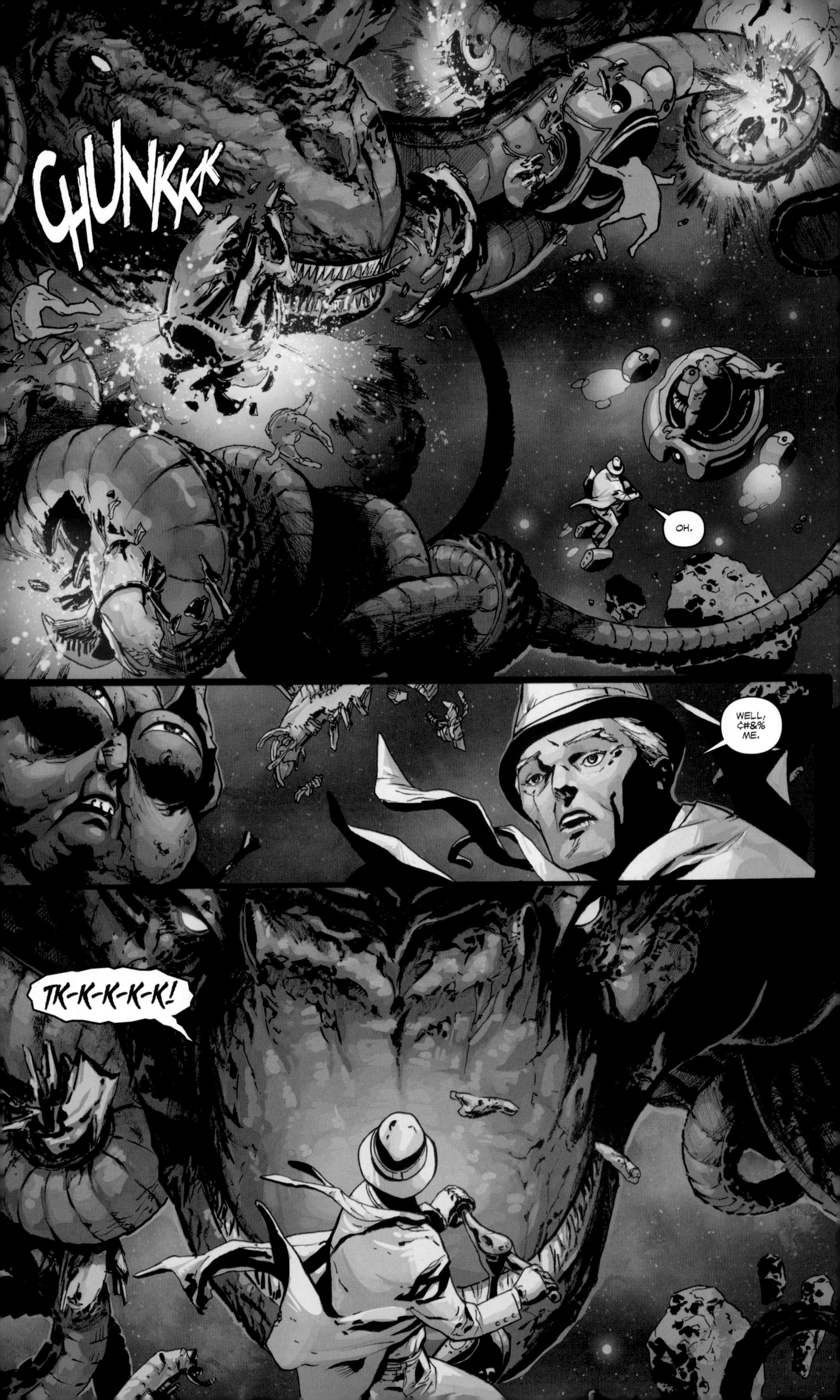
CHUNKKK
OH.
WELL, ¢#&% ME.
TK-K-K-K-K!

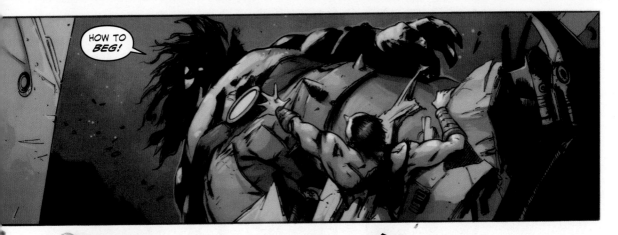

HOW TO *BEG!*

KRUNCH

HEY, FUZZY.

FUN AS IT IS SEEING PRINCESS NAMOR GET A LITTLE HUMILITY--

THESE KIDS AND I REALLY NEED TO HEAD OUT.

IF YOU THINK *TAUNTS* AND *BROAD MISSES* WILL DEFEAT BLASTAAR--

PREPARE FOR A *HARSH*--

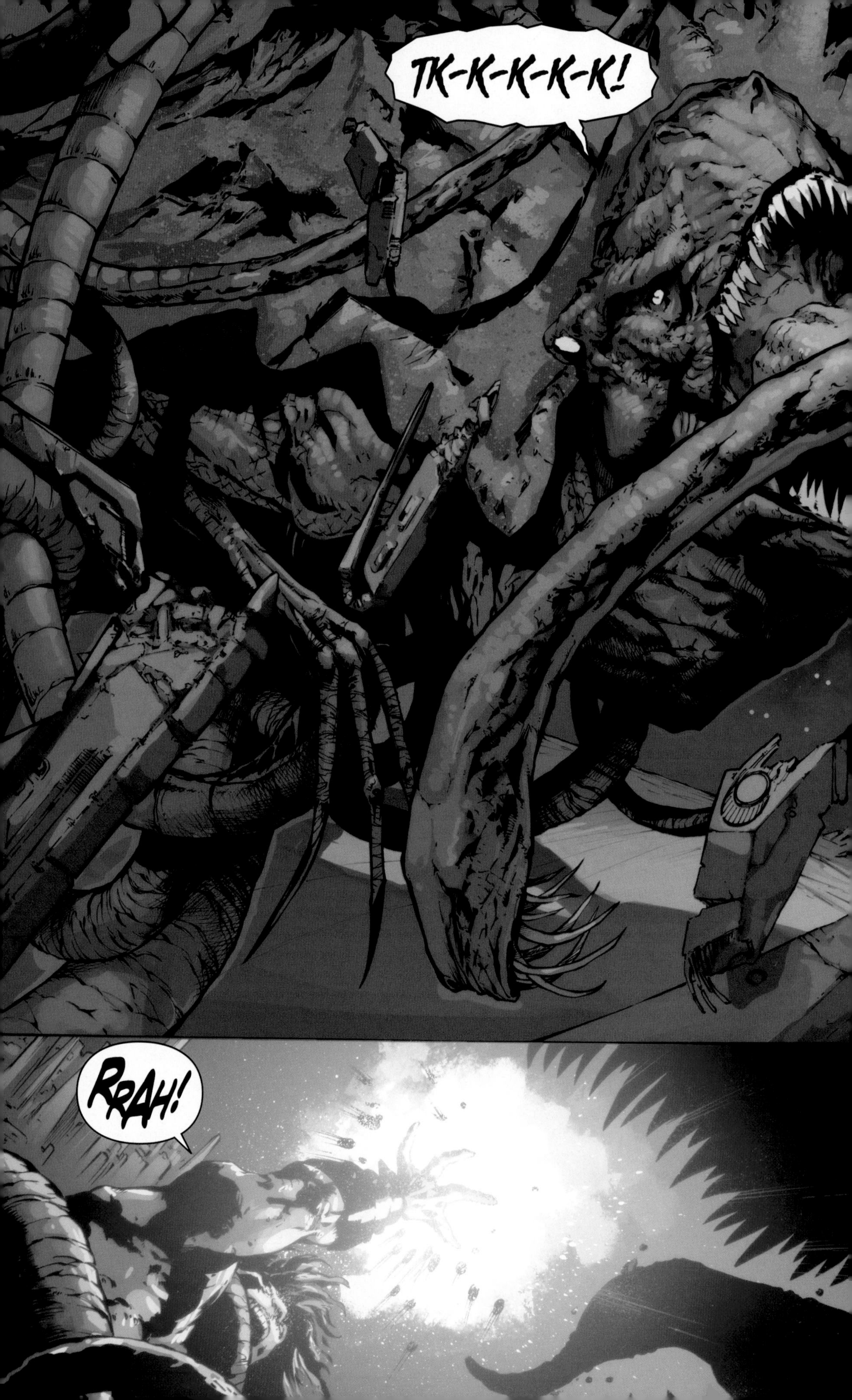
TK-K-K-K-K!
RRAH!

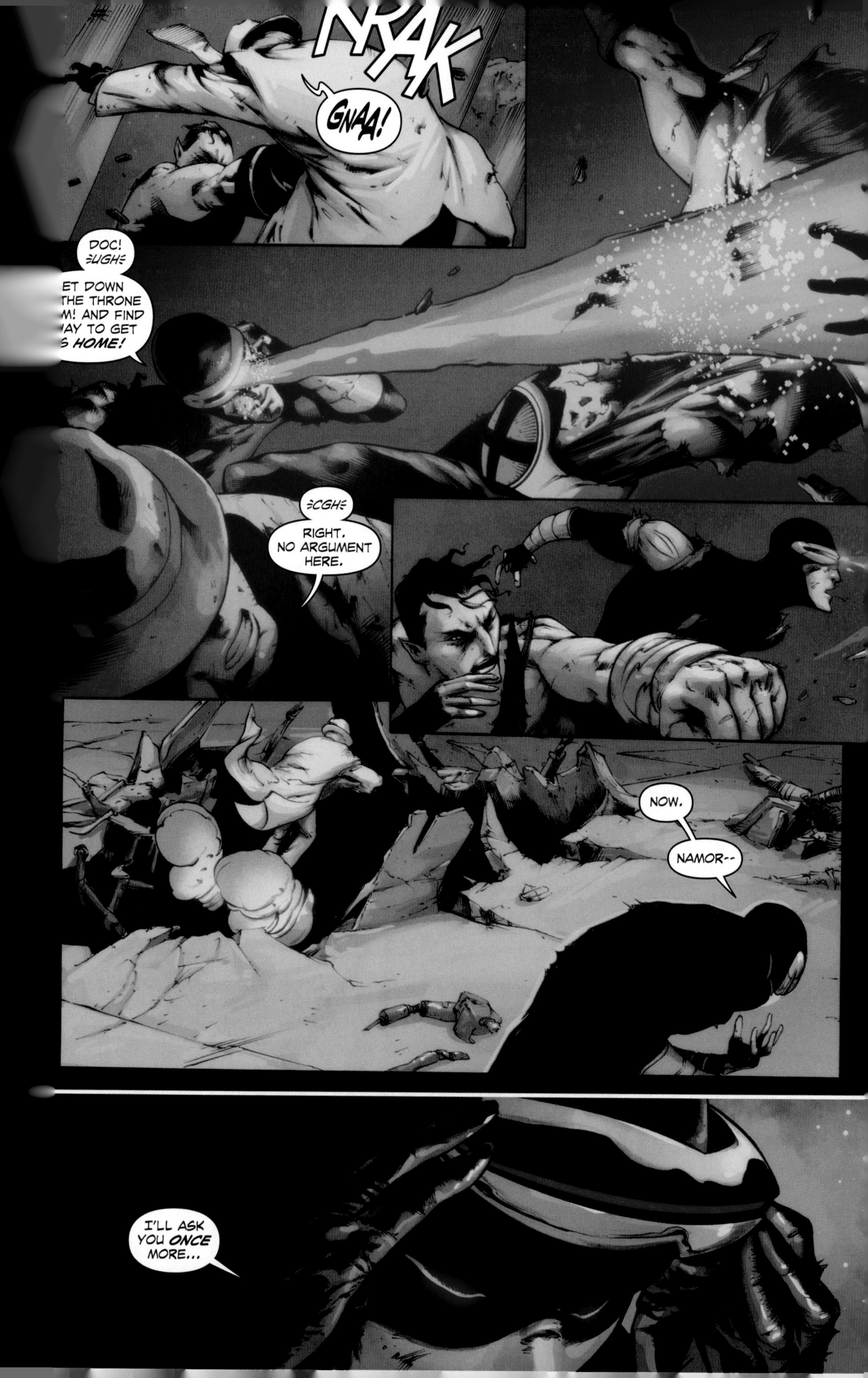

KRAK
GNAA!
DOC! UGH
ET DOWN THE THRONE M! AND FIND AY TO GET S HOME!
CGH
RIGHT. NO ARGUMENT HERE.
NOW.
NAMOR--
I'LL ASK YOU ONCE MORE...

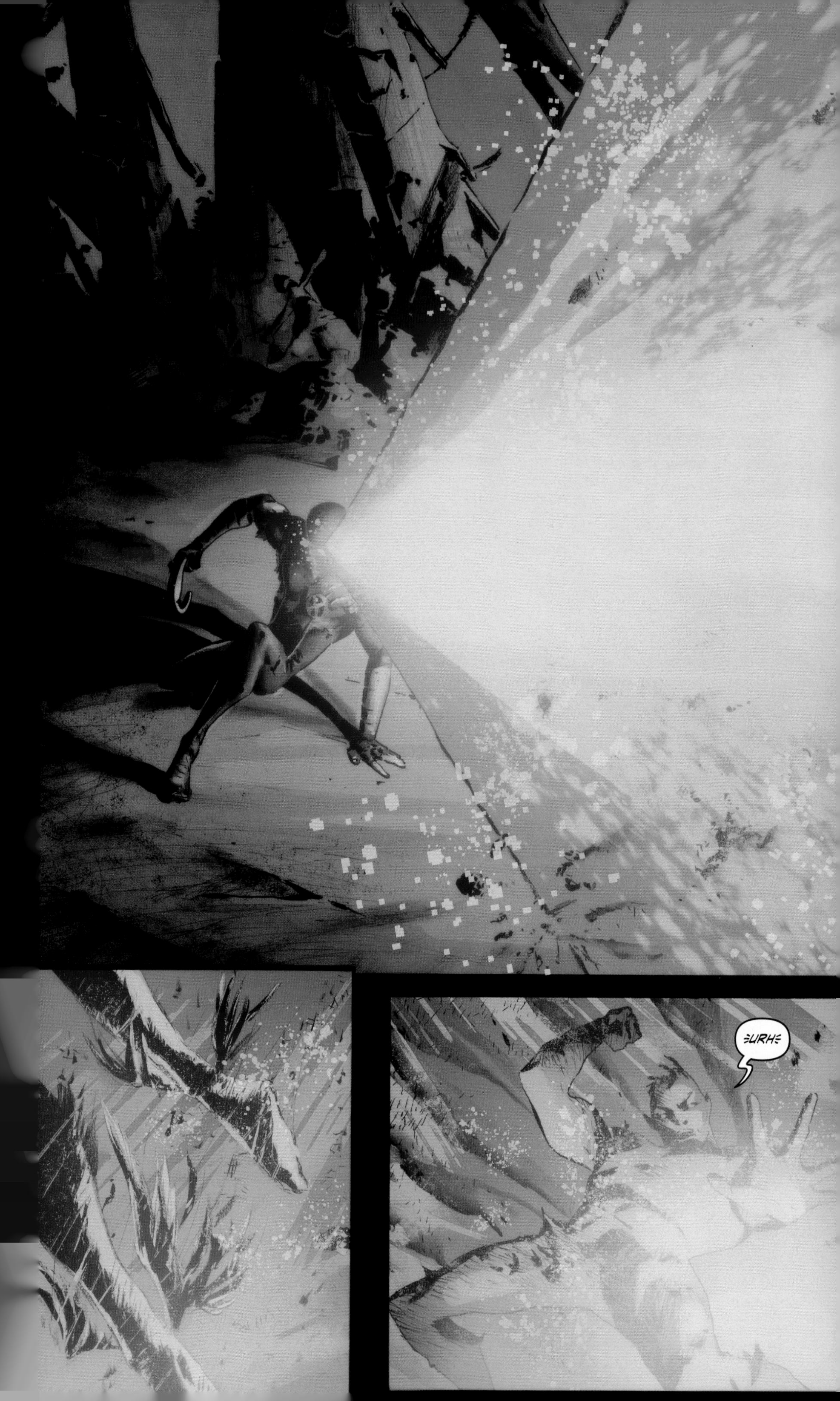
URH

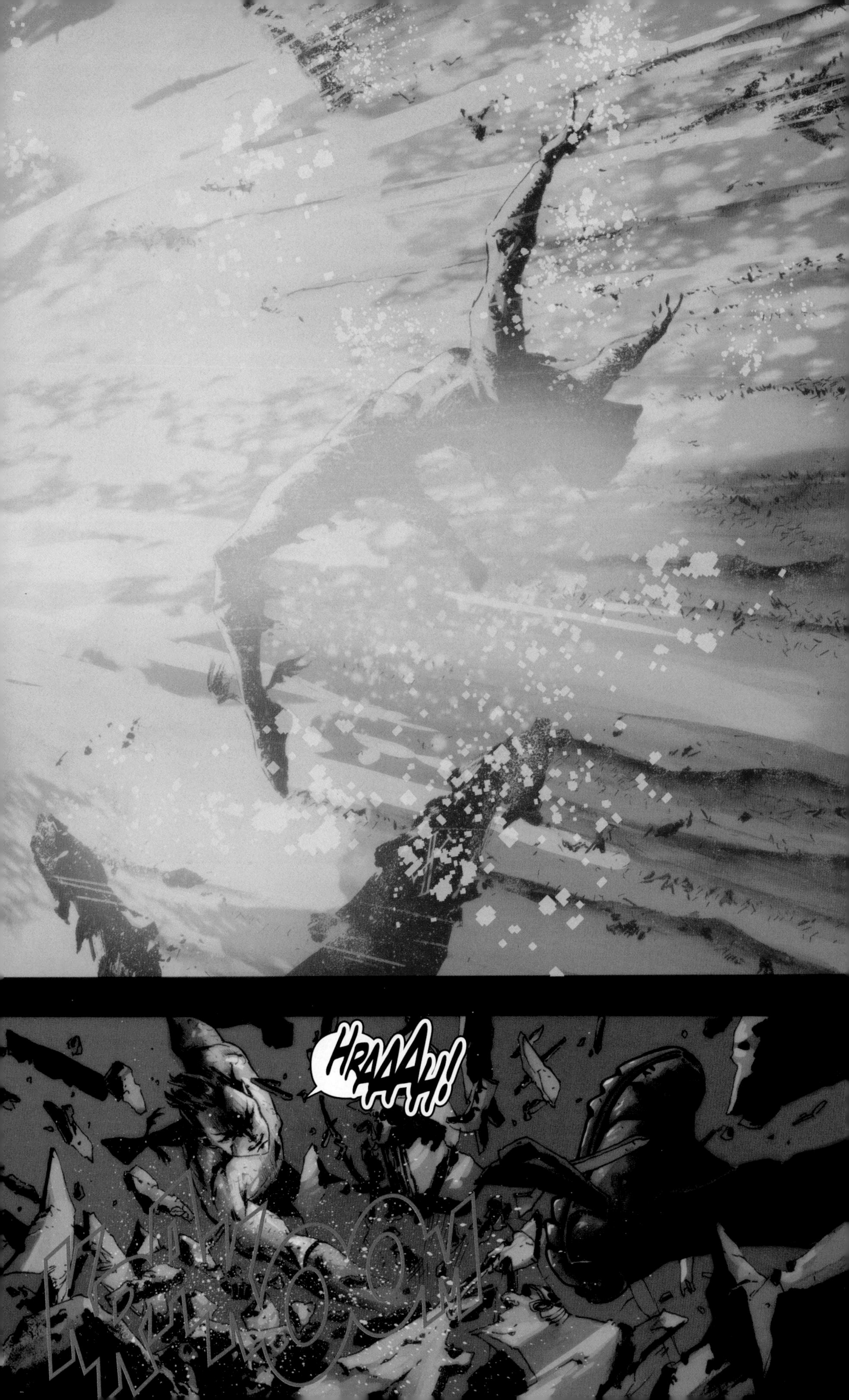
HRAAAH!

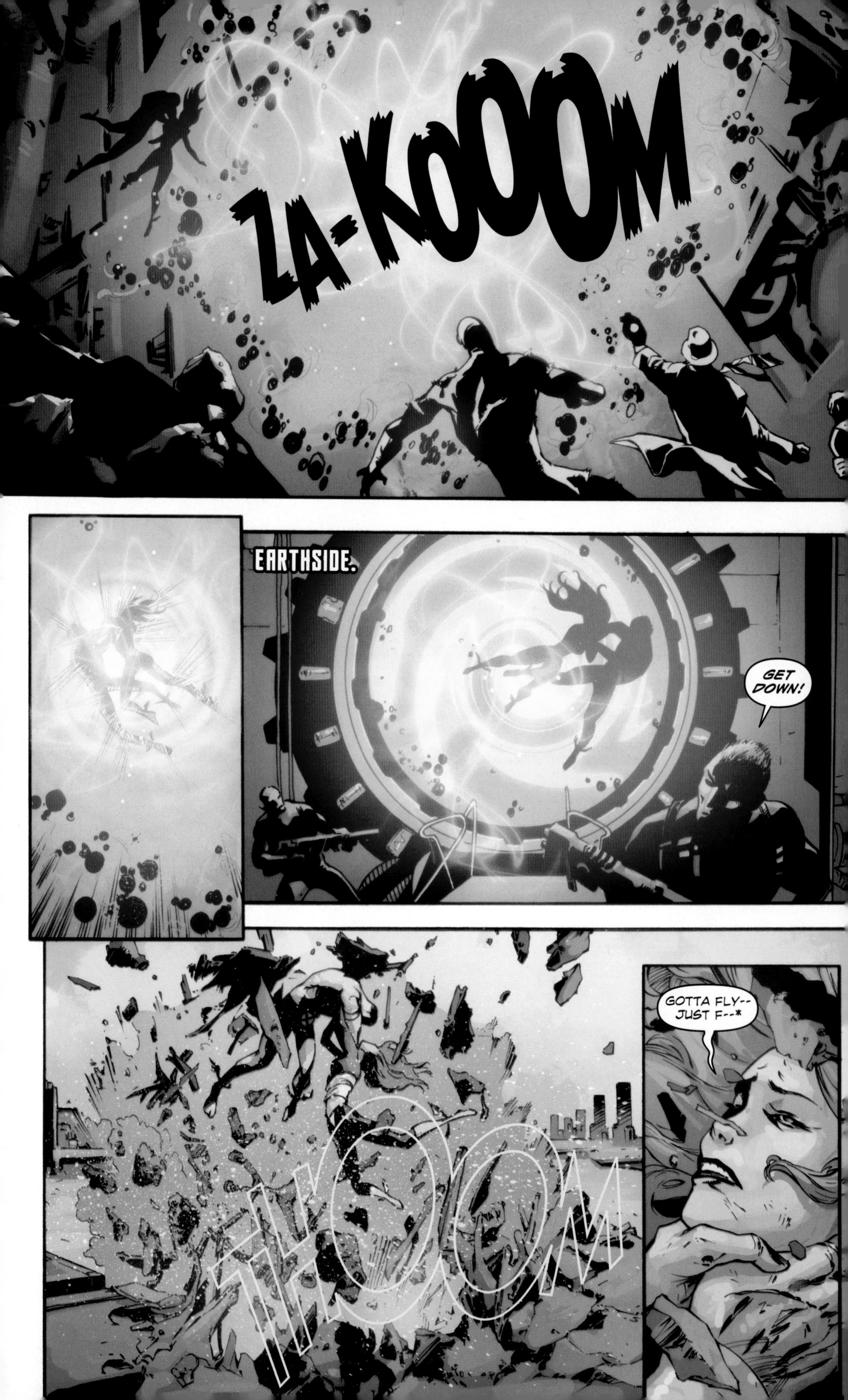
ZA-KOOOM
EARTHSIDE.
GET DOWN!
THOOM
GOTTA FLY-- JUST F--*

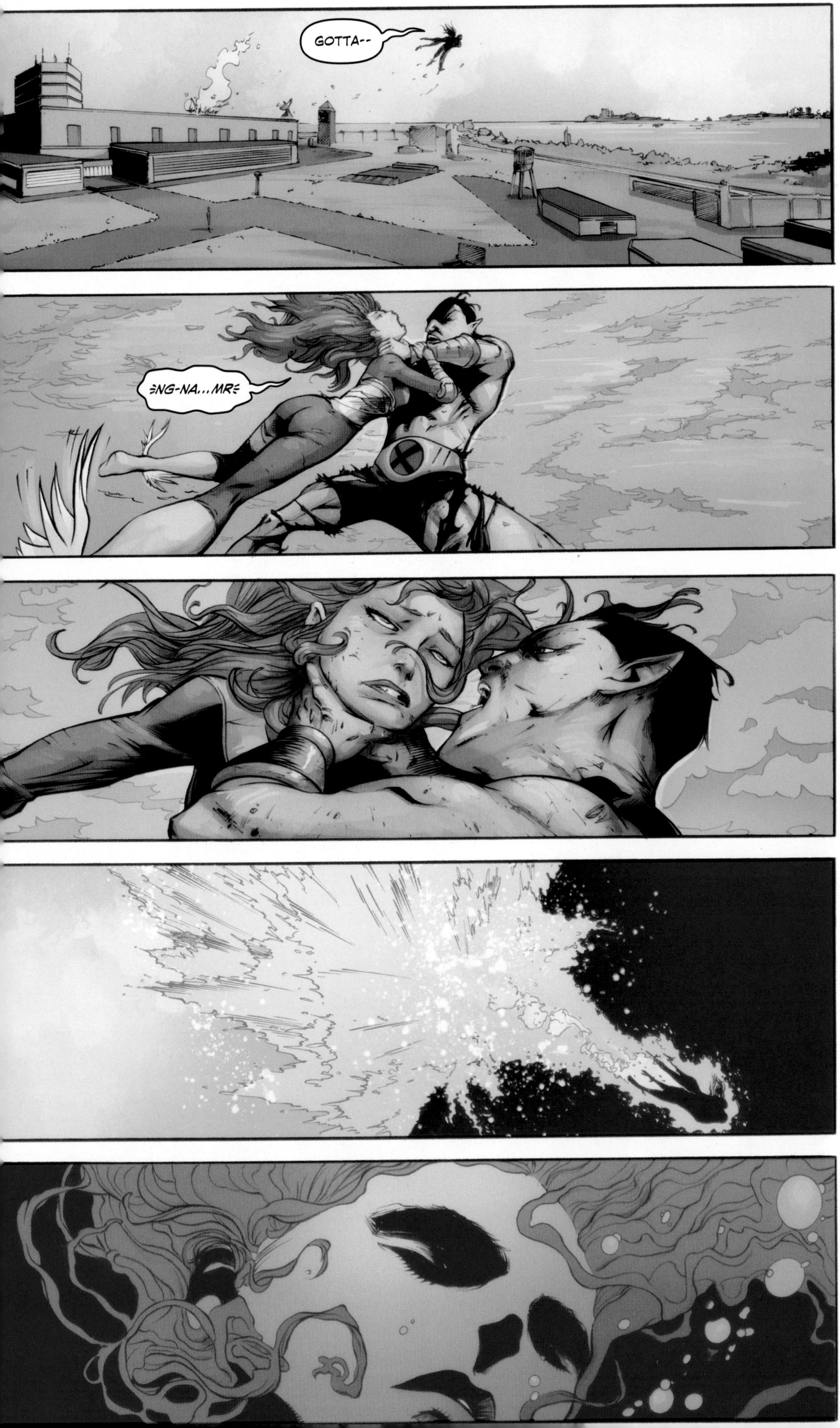
GOTTA--
NG-NA...MR

I ASSURE YOU I AM *FINE!* SO RUN OFF AND CELEBRATE YOUR SUCCESS-- OR I'LL BREAK THE NEXT HAND THAT *TOUCHES* ME.

I THINK YOU'VE DONE *ENOUGH* FREAKING, NAMOR.

AH. ROGERS... I WAS JUST DISMISSING THESE *LAMPREYS* IN ORDER TO--

YOU SAVED ME-- BROUGHT ME BACK FROM THE WORST PARTS OF MYSELF.

WHICH, I SUPPOSE, IS WHAT YOU'VE *ALWAYS* DONE FOR ME.

BUT WHAT I ALL TOO OFTEN FAIL TO SAY IS... I AM *HUMBLED* BY YOUR FRIENDSHIP. AND I *THANK YOU.*

DEAR LORD. I'M GLAD WE MADE IT IN TIME TO SEE *THAT.*

HEH. THAT ALMOST MADE THIS WHOLE DISASTER WORTHWHILE.

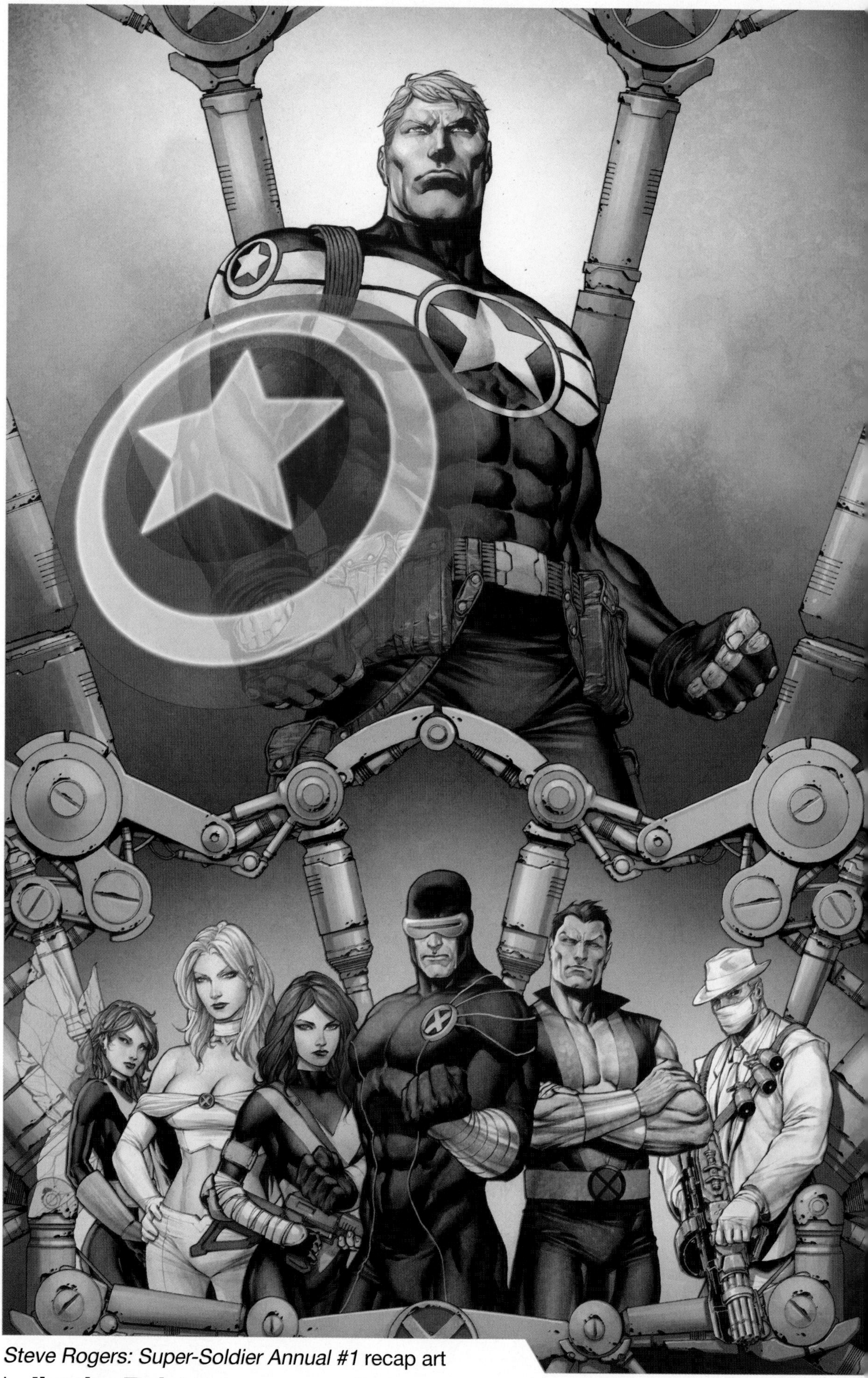

Steve Rogers: Super-Soldier Annual #1 recap art
by **Ibraim Roberson**

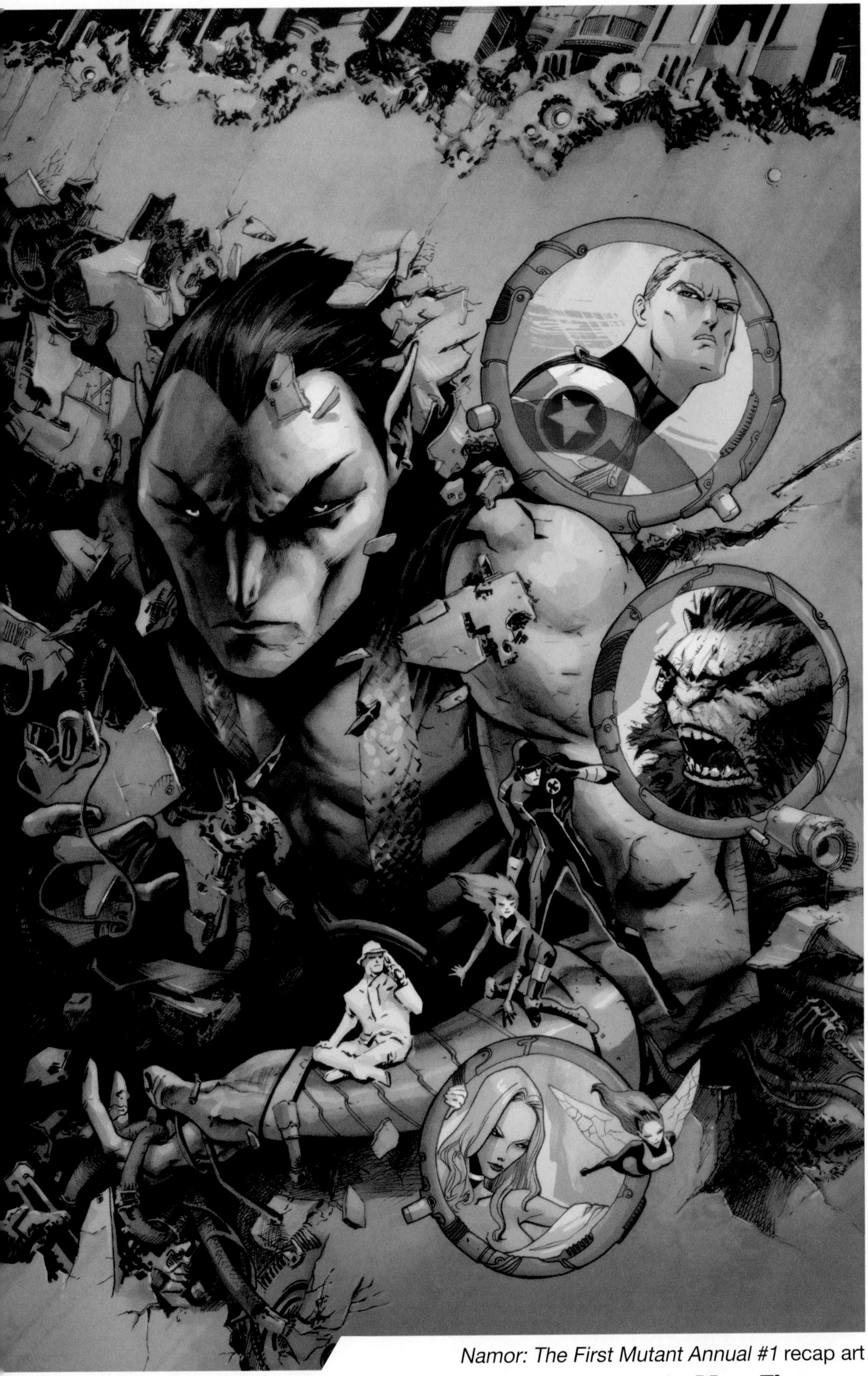

Namor: The First Mutant Annual #1 recap art
by **Max Fiumara**

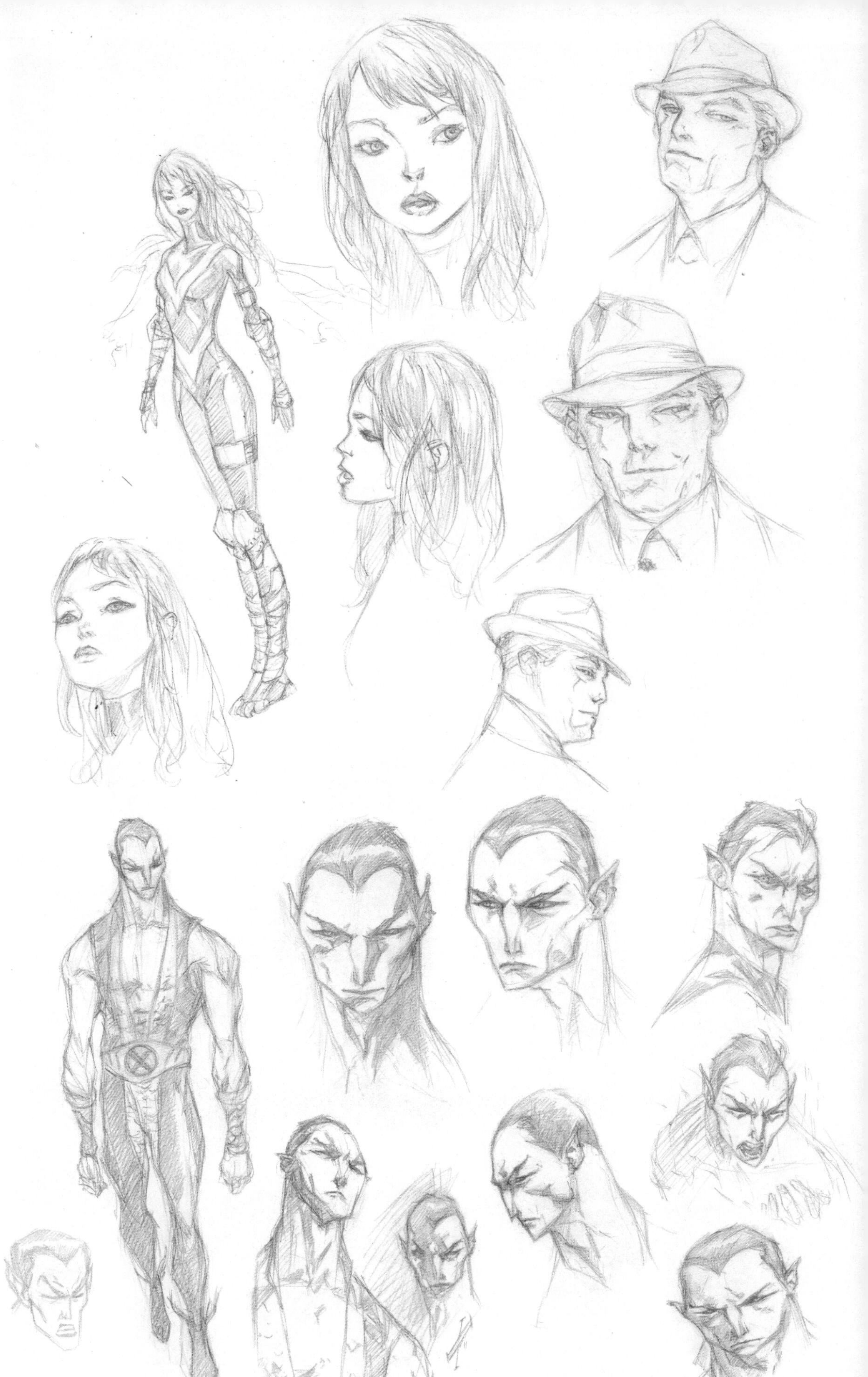

Character studies by **Max Fiumara**

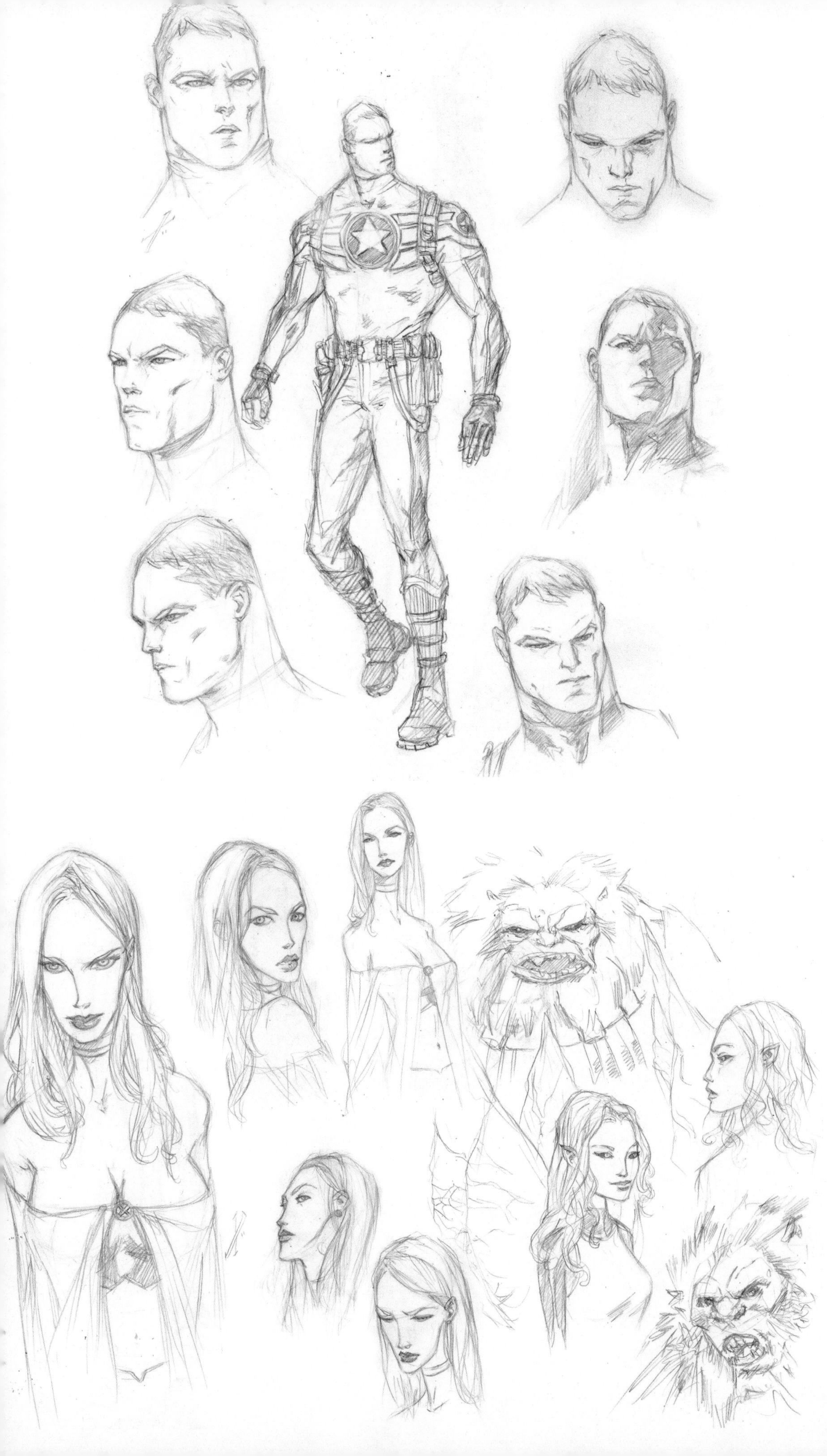

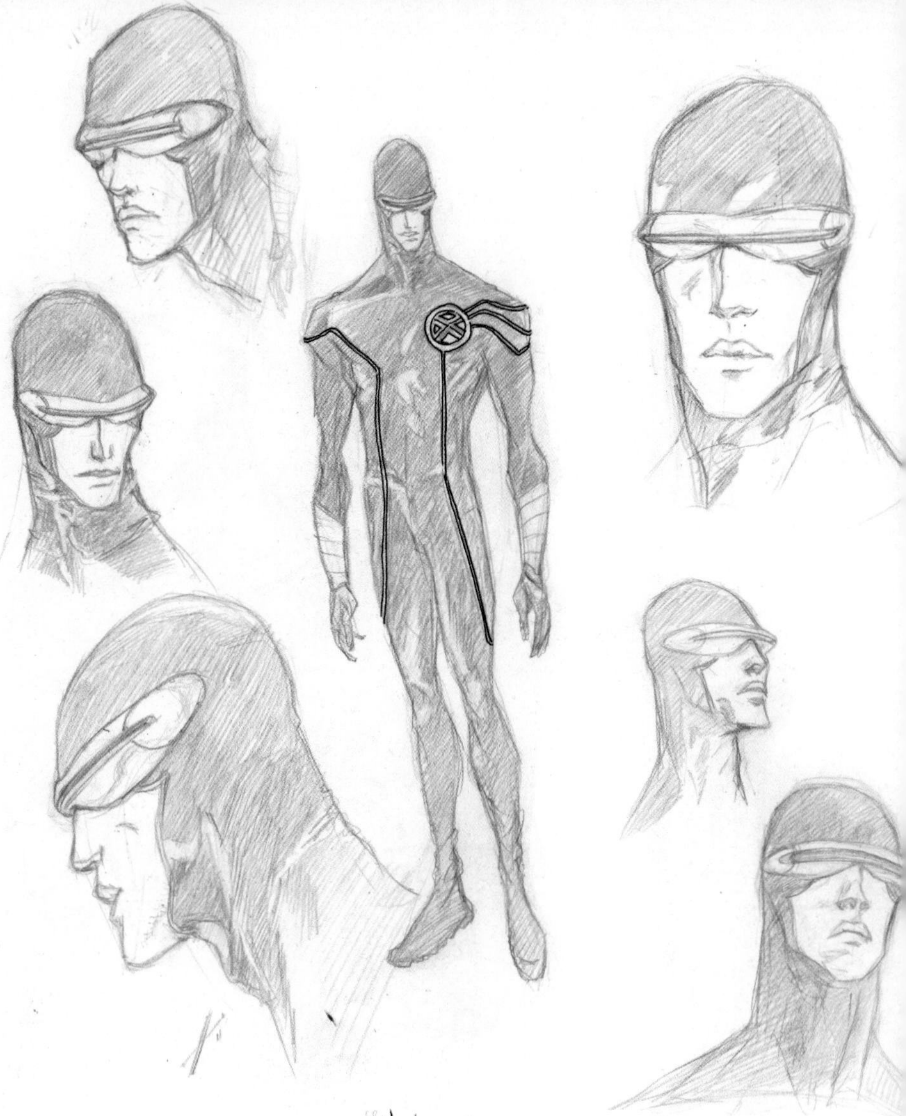

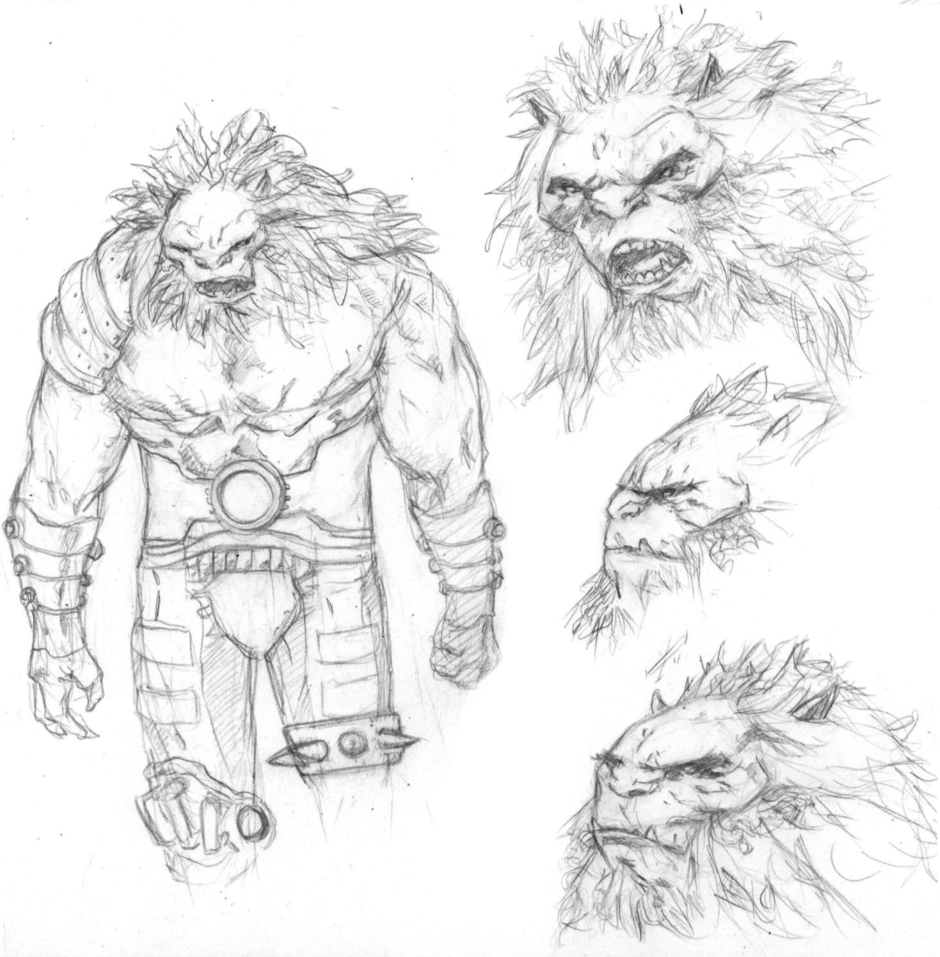